10 Rules for Impossible Projects

Surprising – But True – Advice on How to Successfully Deliver Difficult and Complex Projects

Marcin Dąbrowski

10 Rules for Impossible Projects: Surprising – But True – Advice on How to Successfully Deliver Difficult and Complex Projects

Marcin Dąbrowski
Nowy Wiśnicz, Poland

ISBN-13 (pbk): 979-8-8688-1462-4   ISBN-13 (electronic): 979-8-8688-1463-1
https://doi.org/10.1007/979-8-8688-1463-1

Copyright © 2025 by Marcin Dąbrowski

Managing Director, Apress Media LLC: Welmoed Spahr
Acquisitions Editor: Shivangi Ramachandran
Development Editor: James Markham
Project Manager: Jessica Vakili
Copy Editor: Kim Burton

Cover designed by eStudioCalamar

Distributed to the book trade worldwide by Springer Science+Business Media New York, 1 New York Plaza, New York, NY 10004. Phone 1-800-SPRINGER, fax (201) 348-4505, e-mail orders-ny@springer-sbm.com, or visit www.springeronline.com. Apress Media, LLC is a Delaware LLC and the sole member (owner) is Springer Science + Business Media Finance Inc (SSBM Finance Inc). SSBM Finance Inc is a **Delaware** corporation.

For information on translations, please e-mail booktranslations@springernature.com; for reprint, paperback, or audio rights, please e-mail bookpermissions@springernature.com.

Apress titles may be purchased in bulk for academic, corporate, or promotional use. eBook versions and licenses are also available for most titles. For more information, reference our Print and eBook Bulk Sales web page at http://www.apress.com/bulk-sales.

If disposing of this product, please recycle the paper

*I dedicate this book to Małgosia,
my wife and the love of my life!*

Table of Contents

About the Author

Marcin Dąbrowski has managed and supervised large projects for the world's largest telecommunications groups and banks. He is the co-founder and CEO of People More. He served as vice president on the Comarch management board and COO and vice president on the Ailleron management board. Dąbrowski is the author of *Eternal Delay* (OnePress), *Managing IT Projects* (Apress, 2023), and many international scientific publications (including for ACM CCS DIM 2008, IEEE ICCS 2008), as well as contributions to ITU-T. He is an AGH University of Science and Technology graduate, having majored in electronics, telecommunications, and computer science. He also studied at the Stanford Graduate School of Business and the IESE Business School.

Endorsements

Bold, entertaining, and slightly dangerous—just like all great ideas.

10 Rules for Impossible Projects is the ultimate guide for anyone who loves biting off more than they can chew. A manual for big thinkers with a rebellious streak.

The book dishes out ten golden rules for tackling wild, ambitious, and borderline impossible projects without losing your mind (or your job).

It's part strategy, part reality check, and 100% fuel for dreamers who refuse to settle. Expect failures, expect chaos, but also expect breakthroughs if you play your cards right.

No fluff, no nonsense—just a great read that'll make you want to chase down your dream projects.

Lucas Germanos
Vice President
Zopa Bank

Marcin Dąbrowski's 10 Rules for Impossible Projects is the kind of book every IT leader should keep on their desk—ideally next to a fire extinguisher and a bottle of aspirin.

It doesn't just describe the chaos of large, high-stakes projects—it embraces it with a mix of brutal honesty, practical wisdom, and just the right amount of gallows humor.

If you've ever been handed a project with a fictional timeline, a moving target for scope, and a contract written by people who clearly never planned to deliver it—this book will hit uncomfortably close to home. But more than that, it gives you a way through. Marcin lays out hard-won, field-tested strategies that actually work when theory fails and "best practices" pack up and leave. It's not another cheerfully delusional guide to project utopia—it's a survival manual for the trenches.

Read it, laugh grimly, and keep going.

Ana-Maria Manda
Head of AI Adoption Services Center
SAP

I wholeheartedly recommend 10 Rules for Impossible Projects *to any project manager who has ever felt constrained by traditional methodologies when facing the messy reality of complex projects. Dąbrowski's book is a refreshing departure from academic theory, offering a pragmatic and experience-driven approach to tackling the "impossible."*

What I particularly appreciated was the book's honest acknowledgment of the limitations of conventional project management. It doesn't pretend that certifications and standard processes alone will guarantee success. Instead, it delves into the crucial but often overlooked aspects of project management: client relationships, communication strategies, and the importance of adaptability.

The 10 rules themselves are not just abstract concepts; they're actionable guidelines brought to life by compelling examples and real-world scenarios. The author's insights are both practical and, at times, counterintuitive, challenging you to rethink your approach to project leadership.

Whether you're a seasoned project manager or relatively new to the field, this book provides invaluable tools and perspectives for navigating the complexities of challenging projects and ultimately delivering real value.

It's a must-read for anyone seeking to move beyond theory and master the art of pragmatic project delivery.

Philip Maurer
Distributed Cloud Technology Lead
Google

Having worked on mission-critical projects in highly regulated settings—and as a fellow alum of the Stanford GSB Executive Education Program (LEAD)—I immediately recognized the practical wisdom in Marcin Dąbrowski's 10 Rules for Impossible Projects. This book gets right to the heart of what experienced professionals know but rarely see written down. That is, many projects are set up to fail from day one, and it takes an entirely different mindset to lead them to success.

Marcin lays out ten rules that speak to those of us who've had to deliver under unrealistic timelines, in politically charged settings, and with shifting definitions of "success."

What makes this book unique—and, in my view, necessary—is its focus on external-facing projects where the usual tools, certifications, and frameworks often fail. As Marcin writes, "Project management methodologies don't solve the problems of impossible projects." He's right. The difference-maker is how you think, build influence, manage risk, and lead people when the map doesn't match the terrain.

Marcin and I both spent time in the Stanford LEAD program, where we learned to navigate ambiguity and drive impact through adaptive leadership. That same DNA runs through this book. It's direct, pragmatic, and rooted in experience. If you're in a leadership role where the stakes are high, and failure isn't an option, this book is more than helpful—it's a playbook.

I highly recommend it for senior leaders, project executives, and consultants who've been handed "impossible" and told to make it happen anyway.

Aime Black, EdD, PMP, RBLP-T
Program Management Executive
NASA

Moving from theoretical training to the successful implementation of complex and large-scale projects requires far more than just certification in a project management methodology. Without project implementation experience, the desired success is highly uncertain.

I have read many books on the disciplines of project management and how to ensure compliance with scope, quality, and deadlines. Many large-scale projects suffer from inadequate risk management and thus run into serious difficulties. And this is precisely where this book is a true nugget of gold for me. Marcin not only addresses the main problems that plague projects but also provides us with a guide on how to successfully manage projects through this jungle of substantial issues. While examining the root causes of these problems, he also emphasizes the importance of good relationships between clients and suppliers, as well as within teams. This is a remarkable point for me in times when strategic partnerships between equals are becoming increasingly important.

Thank you, Marcin, for your contribution to successful project execution! For me, this is a must-read for all project managers and decision-makers on both the client and supplier sides.

Moritz Kudalla
Head of Strategic IT Supplier Management
Volkswagen Financial Services AG

10 Rules for Impossible Projects *by Marcin Dąbrowski offers real-world wisdom for managing complex IT projects with confidence. The book provides 10 practical, experience-based rules that go beyond school-book project skills, equipping project managers with the mindset and tools to succeed in challenging environments.*

Marcin emphasizes trust, adaptability, and strong client relationships as the foundation for delivering meaningful results. The focus is on creating value, building momentum, and navigating change with clarity and purpose together with the clients/partners. Rather than striving for perfection, it's about turning difficult projects into success stories. The book is empowering for both seasoned professionals and newcomers looking to lead with impact.

With a mix of humor, honesty, and practical advice, it's a must-read for anyone working under pressure.

This guide shows that even the most impossible (doomed to fail) projects can be delivered with the right approach and mindset.

Dirk E. Witmer
Program / Initiative Manager
UBS Switzerland AG

A must-read for anyone who's ever faced the daunting task of delivering the "impossible."

This book cuts through the noise of certifications and methodologies and gets to the heart of what really matters in complex projects: relationships, pragmatism, and real-world leadership.

As a director in IT portfolio and program management, I found the 10 rules refreshingly honest and incredibly relevant.

Highly recommended for professionals who want to get things done when the odds are stacked against them.

Yavor Nedkov
Director, IT Program and Portfolio Management
Hapag-Lloyd

You must have passion for all that you do. This is also applicable to running projects. Marcin and I have been running projects together and faced a lot of challenges described in this book.

Communication with transparency and clarity is key in our lives and so in projects. Big things need management attention, even involvement, to make them successful.

The best school is the real stuff. Make your hands dirty and grow from project to project. Books like this one are a great source of thought if you have already experienced and faced challenges in projects.

Projects need passion from all involved people, starting from the top.

Christian Laque
CTO
A1 Telekom Austria AG

In his book 10 Rules for Impossible Projects, *Marcin Dąbrowski addresses one of the biggest challenges faced by companies undergoing digital transformation: complex IT projects. Whether in large enterprises or small and medium-sized businesses, such projects—like the renewal and optimization of OSS and BSS systems—are notorious for delays, budget overruns, and draining project managers' energy over an endless period of time.*

*Dąbrowski explores the root causes of these issues. Customers frequently shift priorities mid-project, while system integrators often underestimate the complexity of processes or the specific business models of their clients. Moreover, general management on the customer side struggles to track project progress effectively. The quality of coding by system integrators or IT service providers can often only be assessed by subject matter experts who will later use the system. Given these obstacles, the book's title—*10 Rules for Impossible Projects—*perfectly captures the challenge.*

However, Dąbrowski doesn't just describe the problems; he offers solutions. His book serves as a practical guide for both system integrators, who must place bids in uncertain environments, and companies seeking external support, who risk becoming entangled in never-ending IT projects. By reading 10 Rules for Impossible Projects, *both sides can gain insights to avoid critical mistakes from the outset.*

Written with deep expertise and hands-on experience, this book is a must-read for anyone involved in complex IT projects. Dąbrowski emphasizes the power of sharing knowledge, reinforcing that learning from experienced professionals is key to transforming an "impossible" project into a successful one—delivered on time and within budget.

Rolf Nafziger
Executive Advisor
Deutsche Telekom

Marcin Dąbrowski's 10 Rules for Impossible Projects *offers a practical way to navigate the challenges of very complex projects.*

I have had experience with several impossible projects throughout my career, both as a client and as a vendor, and I believe the straightforward approach described in the book would be very helpful when facing such projects.

The book effectively cuts through theory and focuses on what actually works in real situations. I especially appreciate the practical tips for dealing with tough client relationships and the refreshingly honest advice on handling money issues. The strategies for managing communication problems that often sink projects are clear and actionable, while his guidance on building stakeholder relationships is based on reality rather than theoretical frameworks. The book offers valuable insights on keeping projects financially healthy, which is crucial for professionals in project management roles. Dąbrowski's experience is obvious in his examples and case studies.

This book provides clear, usable guidance for teams facing projects that initially seem impossible to deliver.

Ingólfur Þorsteinsson
CIO
VÍS Insurance

ENDORSEMENTS

10 Rules for Impossible Projects *is a valuable resource for project managers seeking practical strategies to navigate and succeed in complex and challenging IT projects. Its focus on pragmatic solutions, relationship building, and long-term success makes it essential for anyone involved in managing difficult IT projects.*

Marcin Dąbrowski provides a fresh view and actionable advice based on real-world experience, making it highly relevant for project managers. The ten rules cover a wide range of topics, from contract negotiation to financial management, offering a well-rounded guide for practitioners.

This book will help you to deliver impossible projects—enjoy reading!

Dr. Marcus Hacke
Head of Enterprise Marketing & Products
Vodafone Business Germany

In real life, we often find ourselves in situations that don't meet the requirements of theoretical models, or we are forced to attempt the impossible despite all odds. The new book of Marcin Dąbrowski starts where conventional project management methods begin to fail.

Well-structured principles offer pragmatic approaches to significantly increase the probability of success in complex circumstances. It is not intended to compete with academic principles but rather goes beyond them and includes best practice strategies based on broad experience. It considers the dynamics in the interaction of all actors by accepting their real motivation as a factor.

It addresses professionals who are already experts in their field and deal with very challenging projects. The book is a unique source of practical advice to maintain the ability to act no matter what.

Holger Weichhaus
Leiter Qualitätssicherung
Volkswagen Sachsen GmbH

Marcin Dąbrowski offers practical advice grounded in real-world experience, challenging conventional project management methodologies and underscoring the paramount importance of adaptability, proactive problem-solving, and robust relationships.

The book is structured and accessible, providing actionable insights that can substantially enhance project outcomes.

Highly recommended for individuals seeking to navigate the intricacies of challenging projects.

Bruno Delvecchio
EVP Global Delivery
Mycom

After reading the book Managing IT Projects, *I decided to read Marcin Dąbrowski's new book. How do you deliver unrealistic, difficult, or delayed projects? The phrases "pragmatism" and "building relationships" are repeated in this book multiple times, and they are turned into 10 wise and empirically tested rules. Thanks to these rules, this book is priceless not only for running difficult or unrealistic projects but for all projects; I'm sure that the rules can also be applied to projects in your personal life.*

Apart from its vivid language and friendly format, this book strikes a chord in me that relates to my experience and has been at the forefront of my thoughts for a long time, but I have never found a way to reach my consciousness. While reading the book, I realized that I'd often sabotaged myself and made success difficult, usually in goodwill, when I believed in the declarative intentions of both parties and at the same time was completely transparent and believed in mutual open feedback.

Meanwhile, let's be pragmatic, not impulsive.

Anna Streżyńska
CEO, MC2 Innovations S.A.
Minister of Digital Affairs, Poland (2015-2018)

10 Rules for Impossible Projects *is compulsory reading material for people accountable for complex and complicated projects. Decision-makers will find here some mechanisms that influence the effectiveness of change management in organizations.*

As research shows, a significant proportion of complex projects carried out in organizations do not generate the expected business value and do not fit within the initial schedule and budget. However, is this not a natural conclusion? Especially considering that today's companies are complex adaptive systems that—in order to survive in the marketplace—require constant change and maintaining their pace, openness to the external environment, learning, but also unlearning established habits and routines. Project objectives set some time before may be wrong or invalid already at the project's initial stage. Adaptation to current conditions and needs is necessary.

The author skips discussing project management methodologies, which have little relevance in today's business world and do not help to solve key problems. Instead, he offers a pragmatic approach and principles on how to deal with the chaos of change, requirements, expectations, and complexity. At the same time, he seeks effective methods of agreement between the client and the vendor.

In the domestic IT publishing market, one looks in vain for a book on complex projects that focuses on pragmatism execution discipline and reminds us that the most important goal is to solve problems and "deliver the project" to the client.

Sławomir Soszyński
Vice-president, CIO
ING, Poland

10 Rules for Impossible Projects *is an unconventional, original book in which the author makes some bold statements that will probably offend many people in the training, certification, publishing, and*

project management consulting business. He proves with examples that training, certifications, methodologies, and coursebooks are worthless in crisis situations, in moments of facing unrealistic expectations, a toxic environment, a lack of decisiveness, or a constantly changing scope.

Apparently, it's easy to run a simple, well-defined, ideally sized, reliably estimated, and well-sold project with a client who is understanding, patient, well-meaning, and perfectly organized. For those who know anything about running projects, this description sounds like a utopia because, in today's fast-moving world, such projects simply do not exist. Studies show that about 30% of projects are successfully completed, and if we look at huge, complex projects that require the coordination of multiple vendors, this figure drops to 2%. This means that projects described by the author as unrealistic or impossible are our everyday reality, and everyone involved in running a project will sooner rather than later encounter the crisis situations described in the book.

The author has prepared 10 rules for readers, developed on the basis of many years of experience with managers facing unrealistic projects, often referred to as "mission impossible." These principles are not a remedy for all evil and do not guarantee success, but they will help you find your way in stalemate situations and visualize possible paths out of the crisis. Some of the tips are not revolutionary, but in the heat of battle on the front line of project implementation, we often forget about them and let emotions guide us, which only exacerbates problems.

The 10 rules described are tools to be applied at the right moment, which the author puts into the hands of project managers. They include conciliatory tools, such as monitoring the sense of the project, success criteria, applying the Pareto principle (i.e., 20% of the scope can mean 80% of the business value, or launching MVP (minimum viable product) products). There are also those that can be described as applying shock therapy. Their aim is, for example, to shake up the project management, cut off the burden of toxic resources, or apply a strategy that I personally

*describe as grabbing a machete in hand and carving a path to success.
And, as the author points out, you need to tackle the problem here and now
because postponing action is the fastest route to failure.*

*The author also argues that the remedy for delivering unrealistic
projects can be the use of agile methodologies and contracts billed on a
T&M (time and material) basis. The common FT/FP (fixed time/fixed
price) contract gives only a false sense of security, as the reality is always
more complex than that described in the contract provisions. As a result,
a contract that is supposed to guarantee a fixed price and a fixed time
for the delivery of products actually guarantees neither a fixed price nor
a fixed implementation date and either ends in disaster or innumerable
change requests. What's more, the structure of FT/FP contracts often leads
to pathological situations where teams "dig in" at their positions, shift
responsibility for delays, and instead of guaranteeing time and price, we
have a clinch. This is where the rules described in the book can come to
the rescue.*

*I recommend this piece of literature to everyone dealing with project
management tasks. It is worth having it in your bookcase, reading it,
and reaching for it in crisis moments, which no methodology, certificate,
worksheet, checklist, or report can cope with. The effectiveness of the project
manager is crucial because it is the project that is the least profitable period
of the relationship with the client.*

*Personally, I am hoping for a continuation of the series and another
handbook with rules for the implementation of unrealistic projects, this
time in the public sector. Here, the level of difficulty increases geometrically
due to, among other things, the Public Procurement Law, which effectively
restrains the hands of project managers; the obligation to charge contractual
penalties under the threat of violation of public finance discipline; strict
statutory deadlines for implementation, failure to meet which means
acting illegally; or the obligation to launch a product in accordance with
the ToR (terms of reference), without the possibility of redefining it, even*

in a situation where a change in the environment has resulted in a lack of business rationale. Here, any project implemented under the FT/FP formula is already an unrealistic project from the start.

Przemysław Koch
CTO, COO, Member of the Board
VeloBank S.A.

I read another book by Marcin Dąbrowski with great interest. This time, the author touches on two very interesting and relevant topics in the area of IT project implementation. Firstly, "unrealistic projects." Yes, finally, someone has the courage to say that certain projects are not feasible at this time, in this budget, with this team, with this client, with this vendor. What do we do when the unrealistic project has already been created, and we have been entrusted with its implementation? To find the answer to this question, it is worth reading the book 10 Rules for Impossible Projects.

The second theme is the so-called certificate factories that some companies and IT departments are turning into. Again, the author hits the nail on the head, exposing the current certificate fever on the market and the helplessness of people equipped only with certificates when confronted with project reality. One could ask for more on the topic of certificate factories in the area of cloud technologies. I think this would be good material for the next book.

All in all, I highly recommend the read!

Marek Lenz
CIO
Credit Agricole, Poland

Starting to read this book, I expected a considerable amount of practical advice on how to implement projects, and I was not disappointed. Because of his many years of experience running and supervising projects, the author is able to accurately diagnose problems and propose solutions. However, these are not proposals that, like an applied template, will effectively solve the problems, but conclusions to think about and apply in practice.

Certainly, each of the 10 rules needs to be applied in your projects to convince yourself of their effectiveness. With this book, you can start now. The author shares his practical knowledge, thus saving the reader's time.

Bartłomiej Irzyński
CTO, Member of the Board
Vectra

PART I

Impossible Projects

CHAPTER 1

Introduction: How and Why This Book Was Written

Theory is when we know everything and nothing works!
Practice is when everything works, and nobody knows why!

—Professor Jan Miodek

While writing my previous book, *Managing IT Projects,* I wondered multiple times, maybe even constantly, what the readers would think of it. I aimed to present a holistic view of the IT project management environment. I winced when I constantly heard the mantra "projects are delayed" and an implicit complaint that it's the project team's or the project manager's fault. Thus, I wanted to shed some light on the actual mechanisms and reasons behind it. I wanted to reveal the truth. My concern was that by describing the world of project management in an open and direct way, I would expose myself to criticism of the IT community. To my surprise, as time showed, the book was received with positive acclaim. I heard multiple times that, at last, somebody said "how it really was" and that until then, there had been no book on the market depicting the reality of managing IT projects in such a pragmatic way.

© Marcin Dąbrowski 2025
M. Dąbrowski, *10 Rules for Impossible Projects,*
https://doi.org/10.1007/979-8-8688-1463-1_1

I would like to take another opportunity to thank everyone for their kind words and encouragement to keep writing. I hope that my experience has helped you deliver your projects on time, avoided unnecessary challenges and that what I shared was some food for thought.

Many people have asked whether there would be a continuation of the book *Managing IT Projects*. That's why I decided to yield to those requests and write another book on the same subject. For one, I already had some chapters ready that were not included in the first part; another thing is that I wanted to structure my knowledge.

Managing IT Projects revolves around describing the situation as is, revealing the truth, busting the myths around delays in projects, and showing the real reasons for this situation. It is supposed to be a holistic presentation of the projects' business context as well as their life cycle, illustrated by some examples. However, I feel that it lacks focus on specific advice, rules, and principles that each reader (and each of us) should apply when managing customer relationships in a comprehensive way.

This book aims to give you a set of fundamental rules that help to deliver challenging and unrealistic projects. It's worth noting that these rules are agnostic to project management methods. The rules and the methods are meant to complement each other.

In the meantime, my previous book was released internationally under the title *Managing IT Projects. How to Pragmatically Deliver Projects for External Customers.* It got enthusiastic reviews from some prominent people who used to work for companies such as SAP, Audi, T-Mobile, IBM, Google, Proximus, Credit Agricole, Millenium Bank, Cap Gemini, Allianz, British Telecom One Phone or KPN. The foreword to the book was written by Professor Govert Vroom from IESE Business School in Barcelona.

Why You Need This Book

Most project management literature is an encyclopedic compendium of processes, methods, and tools. They tend to explain what the methods are, how to classify them, why some are better than others, why it is so, how to implement a given method, and how to manage projects while sticking to the methodology, method, or process to the dot. You can learn a lot about tools or specific project management areas. There are dedicated handbooks preparing for PMI, Prince2, and IPMA certifications. The problem is, however, that these books are useless when it comes to preparing the future project manager to operate in the actual business environment and with a real client. All you can get is a lot of academic knowledge, which is perfect in some imaginary, ideal conditions in a vacuum. It might be useful when you want to get various certificates, which—by the way—are hardly any proof of having practical skills in the area of project management.

Theoretical knowledge of tools, processes, and methods applied in project management is no doubt useful. But it's only a single element necessary to run projects effectively. Another, arguably even more important requirement is practical experience operating in a business environment. Many actors, including clients, are involved in their processes and ways of working. There are also multiple departments in our own organization. Each of those actors has its own goals and reward systems, which results in modeling or triggering certain behaviors in different stages of collaboration. There are also multiple management levels, including founders, top executives, department heads, line managers, project managers, and team leaders. Moreover, they are present both in the client's organization and our own. All this information can, however, be gathered and described. Sadly, not many books on the market touch upon these issues. In my opinion, there should be more literature about the mechanics of the IT business, instructing project managers on how to operate effectively in this system.

Taking the case further, I must say that most project management books are focused on internal projects, by which I mean projects within your own organization. There are few books looking at the topic of projects run by external clients or even clients' organizations. Both types of projects, internal and external, have their specific characteristics, which means that they should be distinguished from one another, regardless of the project management methods. Therefore, it must be said that there is a negligible number of books about running projects for external clients, which, in my view, makes this book useful.

It is worth pointing out that some projects are likely to be successful no matter what methods are applied, and on the other end of the spectrum, some will fail regardless of the management approach. If project management methods have no decisive influence on the project's success or failure, it is necessary to determine the impactful factors. Obviously, it is a sort of an oversimplification, but it needs to be said that some pragmatic principles need to be adhered to to complete projects and be successful (whatever the client's definition of success may be.) This book proposes some specific rules that should be followed regardless of the chosen project management approach; the methods and the rules are meant to complement each other.

In my view, most authors writing on project management assume that we're dealing with a healthy, well-negotiated, profitable project with no problems whatsoever. Thus, the project manager is empowered, the scope is clearly defined, the timeline is realistic, the client's goals are clear and "set in stone," that there is enough time, resources, support, expertise, and any delays or problems may emerge during the realization of the project. The applied management methods are, therefore, focused on maintaining the status quo. It seems enough to stick to the rules and principles of the chosen method, and everything will end well.

And what if we get a project that is impossible to deliver from day one if we were to stick to the terms of the contract? The timeline is ridiculously unrealistic, the scope is impossible to deliver, or the requirements are unspecified. What if we have no subject matter expertise (as a company), no financial resources to carry out the contract, and so forth? In this case, no project management method will be helpful, mostly because the reasons for the mentioned problems have nothing to do with the method applied. This book presents the rules that should be followed to deliver unrealistic projects despite the difficulties. It is my attempt at busting the myth that for a project to succeed, you must deliver it on time and within the defined scope and quality. There are a myriad of such repeated ad nauseam "golden rules and nuggets of wisdom." If you dig deeper, it turns out that they're not always true or helpful. For instance, consider whether delivering the project as written in the contract will always be a success. Well, not always. It is common for the client to define the scope of the project as early as a year before signing the contract. The project runs for a few years, and only then can the client realize and learn what they really want to achieve. If the project is delayed, does it also mean that it has failed? This is something that has the potential for lengthy discussions.

If we were to stick to the theory, numerous projects would be doomed to fail on the very day when they start or even when the contract is being signed. And these projects are what this book is about. It is about what to do when this is the kind of project you have.

What This Book Is Not

I also owe you a short note on what this book is not, what it does not address, and what you will not find here. A few honest words of self-criticism save time and hopefully spare the disappointment for those who expect something else in terms of content.

10 Rules for Impossible Projects is not a comprehensive body of knowledge nor a handbook designed to describe all existing project management methods. Its aim is not to criticize any specific method or approach. My goal is not to prove that one method is better than all others.

I'm not trying to review or evaluate any project management methods. Just the opposite, my goal is to encourage you to experiment and find your own approach to managing projects.

You will not find a list of the most common mistakes in implementing specific project management methods here. This book presents pragmatic business rules you should follow regardless of which project management method you use. These rules are complementary to any project management approach.

A critical reader could claim that the rules described here will not always be applicable, that the projects I write about are "tough and hard," and that this is not always the case. I completely agree. This book is not about all kinds of projects, especially not those so healthy and well-sold that they can be delivered using any project management method by any team, whether experienced or inexperienced!

This book is only about a selection or a subset of projects that are impossible to deliver, that are tough that people are afraid to even touch, those which were inappropriately sold, delayed from day one, presumably doomed to fail regardless of the project management method used or team assigned to them. Those projects call for an entirely different set of rules. The common project management approaches do not work here. In those instances, clients will not want or tolerate wise clichés or rules such as "It is impossible to run different phases of the project simultaneously and deliver it faster. Everyone knows that you can't produce a baby in one month by getting nine women pregnant." This book is about projects in which clients are not interested in such truisms, but they say in return: "I don't care if it is impossible to deliver. That's the contract you signed."

How This Book Is Structured

Part I, "Impossible Projects," introduces the notion of impossible projects and describes the specific characteristics of such projects, such as an unrealistic timeline, a badly described scope, or too low a price in relation to the workload. It also contains the most common challenges that a project manager and the project team face in such projects. This part also describes the circumstances that led to the creation of such projects and the factors contributing to that. It also talks about who and how contributes to selling those projects first, initiates them, and consequently moves into the firefighting mode from day one instead of working decently and effectively under normal conditions.

In Part II, titled perhaps controversially, but adequately, "Methods and Certifications: BS," you learn why specific project management methods do not solve problems generated by impossible projects and why they not only do not prepare you for facing problems in real life but only drive the training and certification business.

Part III, "10 Rules for Delivering Impossible Projects," covers the book's main message. It describes 10 key rules that any project manager should follow to deliver such a project. The 10 rules are not linked to any particular project management method—these are two independent notions. These rules may seem counterintuitive or unsophisticated. They may seem to stand in opposition to what is usually taught, but they are effective, pragmatic, and useful.

To the Reader

I hope that the knowledge in this book will help you successfully deliver challenging projects, help you brace yourself for tough situations, solve problems pragmatically, and manage projects more consciously. Have a nice read, and good luck!

—Marcin Dąbrowski

CHAPTER 2

What Are Impossible Projects?

If everything seems to be going well, you have obviously overlooked something.

—Murphy's Law

As soon as they begin working on projects, all project managers hear advice on what they should do to successfully run the projects. Each project management approach has its own recipe for success. Everything is laid out in front of you. It's enough to stick to the rules, include every management area, follow the suggested processes, and apply the fully effective tools; you are bound to succeed. Interestingly, there are even clearly defined success criteria for any project. Apparently, it's enough to deliver on time, within scope, and to ensure the required quality. So the question remains: why are most projects delayed, and why do so many fail? It should suffice to invest in training, right? A PMI-certified project manager will certainly cope—or won't they? You can also hire a consultant or a trainer in agile methods. Most companies had come to this conclusion long ago. Many years ago. And yet, the problem has not been solved.

Any experienced project manager also knows that some projects seem easy from the start. Most problems are subject matter issues; solving them won't be a big hassle. It would actually take a lot of effort to make

© Marcin Dąbrowski 2025
M. Dąbrowski, *10 Rules for Impossible Projects*,
https://doi.org/10.1007/979-8-8688-1463-1_2

these projects fail. Some projects need a lot of hard work, but despite all this incredible effort and resorting to various management methods, they remain challenging and often end in failure. Some projects are run perfectly and deliver expected outcomes, but for some reason, they are put on hold. Some are delayed, generating a number of issues and stress, where the scope is delivered only partially, and somehow, it turns out that from the client's perspective, they are considered a success.

I have even come across statements such as "a good project manager knows which project they should accept and which will definitely fail." It's important to point out that nobody is even talking about project management methods!

Thus, you could conclude that there are projects whose success is not significantly affected by management methods. These are the impossible ones that can't succeed according to the project management theory or even to common sense, and they should not even be initiated!

This chapter explains what impossible projects are and what kind of obstacles can be expected while working on them.

Common Problems in Impossible Projects

The list of problems you are likely to encounter in impossible projects is endless. What can you expect, then? The following are the most characteristic, most common, and most fateful.

- Recurring delays

- Expanding or "exploding" scope

- Financial losses

- Lacking resources, no team

- Insufficient domain knowledge in the company

- Undefined or constantly changing project goals

- Unfavorable or even hostile attitude on the client's side

- Constant client pressure to deliver more and better (regardless of the project's scope)

- Clients avoiding decisions

- Astonishing, destructive, or unpredictable decisions or actions on the client's side

- Incurring penalty charges or threats to put the project on hold or to terminate the contract

While dealing with an impossible project, you usually need to stick to a timeline with deadlines that are objectively impossible to meet. You can't make up for lost time. Each project team member is aware that there is no way to deliver the scope within the required time. The problem of "exploding" scope is very common. Step by step, as the features are unpacked, they turn out to be more complex than was previously thought, with much more to deliver and the workload entailing much higher costs that had not been anticipated. You're losing money day after day. The management is annoyed, the team shrinks, and the budget is reduced. This, in turn, leads to negative feedback in the form of longer delays, escalations, and, consequently, even worse working conditions for the project team.

To add insult to injury, the goal of a project like that is subject to constant changes. The client changes the priorities, and thus, the work becomes ineffective. To make matters worse, the client, despite the challenges in the project, demands more for less and adds new features that don't seem to have been included in the initial scope of the project. When you try to talk and solve problems, it turns out that there's no one available on the other side, and people avoid responsibility. In projects like that, the situation often escalates to a degree where the client threatens to incur penalty charges, sometimes even does so, or halts the project altogether and terminates the contract.

I've heard a comment that "not all projects are like that." Yes, indeed. The case described may seem exaggerated and overly pessimistic. However, projects like that are not infrequent. It's sad that so little is written about it. This book does not focus on simple projects, which are bound to succeed anyway. It focuses on the tough ones, those whose problems are not easily solved by applying well-known project management theory.

The Characteristics of Impossible Projects

What are the characteristics of an impossible project that result in the problems described earlier? The following list includes the most important ones.

> **An unrealistic timeline, deadlines impossible to meet**: This is an objectively unrealistic timeline, regardless of the project management approach you use or the unlimited resources you have. This kind of timeline is neither a result of the project team's errors nor of problems encountered during the course of the project. This kind of timeline is sort of "inherited" from the contract. Generally and frankly speaking, someone at the company decided that the terms of the contract were acceptable and subsequently signed the very contract. This leads to a situation in which delivering the scope on time is impossible.

> **Too general, undefined, or improperly defined scope of the project**: Practically speaking, the client's demands align with the contract's terms. Therefore, if the scope of the project is unclear or

too generally defined, it always leads to a situation in which you need to deliver more than was initially planned.

The scale of the problem depends on a multitude of factors, including the client's attitude and the discrepancy between the project deliverables and the client's expectations. Yet, vendors also make some assumptions about the scope and cost of the contract. Their estimates very often turn out to be inaccurate. The reasons for that are also complex, including the missing features of the product (if it even exists), insufficient domain knowledge, inadequate pre-sales analysis, and so forth.

Too low revenue, wrong financial terms of the contract, too low revenue in relation to the workload: The project that is sold properly is likely to succeed. The project that is sold badly results in losses (even though it can be considered a success by the client.)

One of the most prominent characteristics of impossible projects is their bad financial condition. It is never linked to the project manager's or company's "excessive spending." We're talking about a situation where the project costs much more than expected, more than a well-estimated project of this kind should cost. The consequences are far-reaching and pitiful: a lack of resources, no competence, low priority within the organization, assigning people to other projects, delays, and client escalations, to name just a few.

Project business goals that are defined too vaguely, generically, badly, or not defined at all: It might seem that a defined scope is enough to determine the expected outcome of the project. Unfortunately, there are situations where the client (despite having signed the contract) has not given enough thought to the business case and what they actually want to achieve. The consequences can be tragic.

Even a well-run project in which the expected outcomes are delivered can be completely reorganized or put on hold. There comes a day when the client announces the change in priorities, and the scope changes accordingly, not to mention the timeline. Moreover, situations like that can happen several times in the same project.

I'm reminded of a project where the client, out of nowhere, came up with a spontaneous idea to deliver the frontend features with a different out-of-the-box solution (from a different vendor) and focus the project on the backend part only. It's not hard to imagine how such decisions affect individual people, the team, the project, and our business (as a vendor).

Unrealistic assumptions on the vendor's side: Various assumptions that were not thought through, wrong, or made in contradiction to the subject matter experts' opinions and didn't reflect reality. Someone assumed that the product was 50% ready when, in fact, it didn't exist at all. Someone supposedly agreed with the client that the scope, some features, migration, or integration would be simplified, but there is no trace of this agreement in the contract.

No good or even good enough relationship with the client, the project sold against the will of some stakeholders on the client's side: It's not often talked about, but there are projects sold against the will of some important people or groups on the client's side. It's one of the worst situations for the team and project manager. It results in hostile activity or even a sort of "silent boycott" on the client's side. Sabotaging discussions, challenging agreements, putting off meetings, constant criticism, and looking for issues. Projects like that often fail no matter what project management approach is used.

Improperly written contract, no defense mechanisms against the client's unreasonable demands or penalty charges: Running a project based on an inappropriately written contract is extremely hard, especially when there are no adequate provisions on the scope control, no procedures for delays, and incurring penalty charges. You end up in a situation where everything depends on the client's attitude, their honesty or lack thereof, where in some doubtful circumstances you could "put up a fight" for what's justified, you can't do anything and need to succumb to the client's wishes even when you seem to be in the right.

You may find yourself in a situation where the client delays the project, but according to the contract, the vendor can bear the consequences. You may deliver a milestone, but the client keeps adding to the scope and changes the criteria, and your hands are tied. Some clients approve the correctly delivered system depending on whether the contractor agrees to deliver some extra scope, and some even withhold payments of properly issued invoices until the extra scope is delivered.

A badly written contract puts the vendor and the project manager in a defensive position from the start. In some extreme cases, vendors are forced to keep delivering unprofitable projects without any possibility to stop the losses and terminate the contract,

No right fit between the vendor and the client/ different mentality and work culture: Differences in work organization, mindset, management processes, decision-making policies, approach to solving problems—all this leads to tension, escalation, and delays. If your organization runs all projects in an agile way, it will be difficult to work with a client who has a very rigid approach to making decisions and changes, where everything has to be carefully planned, and key decisions are processed for months in a hierarchical order.

When the project is run in a country with a significantly different national culture, it can take months to understand the client's approach. What's more, certain business practices may be totally unacceptable for you, such as delaying payments for correctly issued invoices, withholding the approval of analyses and documentation until the working system has been approved, and so forth.

The client who is not well-prepared for the project: It's often the case that the client is not prepared for the project. There are no domain experts, leaders, or people responsible for particular areas. There is not enough subject matter expertise. The client is not able to deliver the artifacts that the vendor needs. There is not enough knowledge about the internal systems that are supposed to be replaced or integrated with the newly developed systems or features. On the client's side, there is no plan for adapting the organizational structure to the decision-making process. It's very hard to run a project in an environment like this,

Unstable business environment: A risky business situation that you entered by signing the contract, which can include an approaching M&A process on the client's side (mergers and acquisitions, which means buying other entities, consolidation, or selling a part or the entire business), changes in the board or the management team, approaching strategic decisions in relation to choosing the key contractors. Running a project in conditions like these is usually unpredictable.

Whether the project is run properly or not does not really matter. If, for example, the client acquires a business with an up-to-date IT system that overlaps the scope of your product, your project is highly likely to be put on hold. If, on the other hand, the client is preparing to sell the business, they can halt all investments (including your project) if they decide that they do not contribute to raising the value of the business.

An impossible project may be defined only by some of the preceding characteristics. It's often enough to encounter one or two to make the situation so complex that completing the project seems unattainable. Let's take, for example, the most common type of an impossible project, which is a situation in which the sold product is either far from complete or nonexistent. Sounds familiar? You are supposed to deliver a system that you don't have. What's more, this task has a deadline. The difficulty is that there is not enough domain expertise. When the contractor does not understand the domain or the client's expectations, it manifests in a badly or generically described scope. The natural consequence of this situation is an overly optimistic approach to estimates and prices that don't cover the costs. That, in turn, leads to a lack of financial resources to pay for the team, delays, conflicts with the client, escalations, penalty charges, and so forth.

To Sum Up

There are numerous examples of impossible projects. Replacing IT systems at the client's company in which the delay was as long as three years and exceeded the cost several times. Migration to the new IT platform where the client got only a third of the scope and the project was delayed by two to three years before being stopped by the client. Developing a new IT platform for one of the clients was also delayed by a few years, and the cost significantly exceeded the initial estimates.

Running an impossible project is extremely difficult and often exhausting for both the client and the vendor. It's a very challenging relationship that generates complex issues with no simple solutions. Moreover, the theory of project management does not help much here. It can come as a surprise that in this type of project, the project manager abides by the rules of the chosen methodology. You could say that they work impeccably, but the project remains impossible!

So, if impossible projects are actually detrimental to all parties, it's worth asking questions about why they are even created in the first place, where they come from, and whether they can be effectively run. You'll find the answers to that in the following chapters.

CHAPTER 3

How and Why Impossible Projects Are Born

A silly thing is most dangerous when there are reasonable arguments to support it.

—Tadeusz Kotarbiński

You already know what an impossible project is, what problems it usually generates, and what its characteristics are. This chapter looks at the circumstances in which such projects are created, what contributes to their creation, who and why drives the sales of such projects, and who initiates them, leading to operating in the firefighting mode from day one.

As could be expected, projects become impossible already in the sales phase when the most important parameters are decided, including the project objectives, mutual expectations, expected outcomes, scope, timeline, quality criteria, and approval procedures. When the project's blueprint is created, the most significant risks are identified, and they will surely materialize in the form of challenges and characteristics described in the previous chapter. If, for instance, the timeline outlined in the contract is far from the actual capabilities of the supplier, it's unreasonable to expect the project to be delivered on time. The delay is a foregone conclusion. Likewise, if the system being sold does not exist yet, or the scope of the project is too vaguely described, the challenges are also to be expected, including the increased project costs.

To understand more clearly which factors contribute to creating impossible projects, you need to analyze two important aspects: the sales process and the environment in which sales processes are executed.

Environments That Are Fertile Ground for Creating Impossible Projects

The sales process involves a lot of parties whose aim—in theory—should be the same, who should act like partners and in full transparency. Good contracts and healthy projects are created in a work environment where people focus on the same goals and where decisions are evidence-based. Problems arise when dealing with multiple groups of interest or actors, and each of them tries to maximize their benefits and achieve their own goals, which are not necessarily compatible with the project objectives. What are the actors involved in the sales process, why do they act as they do, their behavior patterns, and what are the tensions and conflicts?

You can start by dividing the future users of the system and the management (on the client side). The users want to maintain the status quo; they're afraid of change, and they usually want the new system to be a copy of the current one to keep their way of working.

On the other hand, the management wants to introduce changes to new business processes, increase efficiency, and lower costs, which may lead to (and often does) layoffs and decrease the users' perceived level of safety. Considering all this, it's easy to understand the users' attitude to defining the scope during the sales process and the subsequent project delivery. Obviously, they will try to stick to the current environment and ways of working.

It's clear that however the features of the new system are defined, users will be fighting daily to ensure that the upgraded, modern tools resemble the ones used so far. There will be challenges with increasing costs, delays, conflicts, delivery of the features that were not a part of the initial scope, and so on.

From the management's point of view, the important parts of the project definition are the objectives, outcomes, corporate KPIs, and transformation goals. The problem is, however, that in the sales and negotiation phase, there are far too many unknowns to get down to details. Therefore, the contract usually contains some declarative goals.

If you take into consideration the fact that the contract is most often negotiated at the management level, and the project's outcome is for the users, it's only natural that the problems mentioned earlier will surface during the delivery phase. There's little understanding on the client side about what and why their management agreed to—users have their own vision of the new system, one person defines the requirements for the project, it is managed by yet another, and someone else altogether will be responsible for approving it. The scope and costs are constantly rising, and deliveries are delayed.

The actors can also be generally divided into the client party and the vendor party. Their goals should be partially the same and partially different for obvious reasons. It is clear that the vendor wants to sell the product for a higher price, ensure sufficient time to complete the work, and offer the existing version of the product without adding any additional features. The vendor does not want to accept accountability for the areas they have no control over.

Conversely, the client wants to buy the system at a lower price, get it delivered sooner, make the vendor take full accountability, coordinate the project on both sides, and deliver the system to any third party. These contradicting goals are, to some extent, natural and objective. The key thing is that both the client and the vendor should care about the transparent and honest assessment of the system's completeness and thoroughly analyze the actual timeline and terms of the contract, which ensures maintaining a partnership on equal terms during the delivery phase.

It is often the case that during the sales process, the goals that should be convergent to some extent are unreasonably twisted to achieve the particular goals of the negotiating parties. There are vendors who deliberately hide some facts and agree to unrealistic terms to get the deal. There are clients who prefer to define the scope vaguely and refrain from the initial requirement analysis so that the project does not turn out to be more costly or extended in time. These actions have far-reaching and painful consequences. The projects supposedly cost "more" and last "longer," while in reality nothing has changed. From an objective standpoint, the scope of the project was known from the start. Both parties only pretended that things were different.

Finally, you can identify different actors inside the client's and the vendor's organizations. On the client's side, they include the so-called business, the IT department, the purchasing department, the legal department, and the security department, to name a few. The vendors are the sales and pre-sales consulting department, R&D, implementation, and maintenance departments. Even though each company may be structured differently, it is important to point out that various units are treated in this discussion as actors influencing the creation of impossible projects. Both on the client's side and on the vendor's side, each of the actors may have their own goals, mostly determined by the assessment, compensation, and bonus systems. A model salesperson aims to finalize the contract, often at the cost of compromises that won't be accepted by the implementation department (too low price, too ambitious timeline, too ambiguous penalty clauses).

Yet, while estimating the project, the R&D and implementation departments quote a cost so high that the sales department finds it difficult to make the offer competitive. On the client side, the business aims to obtain the best possible system (and rightly so) in terms of its functional features and technology, which in turn usually negatively affects the scope, price, and timeline. The IT department needs to deliver the project, so their goal is to make the implementation fast and easy. Each department may generate some extra requirements, which increases the cost and influences the schedule.

Unless the goals and interests of all the mentioned actors are synchronized, you end up with an explosive mixture at the root of any impossible project. Some are afraid of changes and try to avoid them; others want to implement them. Some want to sell the project at a low price to achieve the sales targets and earn a bonus, while others want to sell it at a higher price to produce higher margins and earn their bonus (calculated using a different scheme). Some force a low price and an unrealistic timeline to make a business case for the project, while others promise their organization a cheap project and a "safe" (but, in fact, unrealistic) timeline to sign the contract faster. Some try to add clauses that will keep the company safe, while others try to enforce the contract that will make it possible to control it from a legal point of view.

The contradicting goals and interests of particular actors and their respective evaluation, compensation, and bonus systems create an environment that lacks transparency and partnership while designing the basic parameters of the future project: its business objectives, goals, scope, timeline, and mode of delivery.

What Purchasing Processes Usually Lead To

You already know that the sales process involves a number of parties whose interests are often contradicting. From the sales process perspective, it is important that the clients want a shorter timeline, a lower price, and a generally defined scope because that allows them to put pressure on the supplier and demand more features at the same price. They often avoid agile methods and T&M contracts (time and material) because they fear losing control over the project scope and cost. They often reject the idea of initial analysis (before the project starts) to avoid the situation in which the project turns out to be more complex, longer, and more costly. For this reason, clients opt for the fixed price/fixed scope approach, where the scope and the cost are supposedly known upfront.

On the other hand, vendors want to sell their products and services at a higher price. There must be a clear and objective method of price verification. Vendors also want more realistic and comfortable timelines, which may be too long from the client's point of view.

Most mature organizations implement purchasing processes to verify the bidders. In theory, their outcome should be an objective evaluation of the vendors, their products, deadlines, and prices. Generally speaking, only a limited number of bidders are invited to the purchasing process. Then, the first version of commercial offers is collected. They undergo evaluation. After that, the best offers are shortlisted. More detailed information is required. Finally, there is another, even shorter list of bidders who are invited to the negotiation phase. In theory, the purchasing process should end with the client having a clear view of the market and a full understanding of the pros and cons of the offers provided, thus enabling them to select the best proposal based on the predefined criteria.

In practice, though, purchasing processes have faults and weaknesses that often lead to inadequacies. They are structured so that the offers are compared in documents. Thus, some important aspects are neglected, such as whether the product meets the requirements, how much it will cost to customize it, what the actual scope is, how long the project will last in reality, and how much it should cost.

Purchasing processes are often reduced to reading promises printed on paper. This leads to a lot of dishonest behavior. Vendors know what they should do at every step of the process. The practices include artificially lowering the price, shortening the timeline to an unrealistic degree, and promising non-existent products (assuming that all of this can be somehow addressed later). Clients also know how to exert pressure on vendors to get more value, to get it faster, how to write contracts to enforce an extra scope, what clauses to include to incur penalty charges for even the slightest delay, and so forth.

Interestingly, both parties are fully aware of the problems mentioned and of the dishonest practices, yet contracts for impossible projects are still signed! The situation will stay like this as long as purchasing processes focus on comparing offers only on paper.

Proper purchasing processes should focus on the project subject matter, objectives, and outcomes, not the low price and short timeline. Low prices hardly guarantee that the project will be delivered at the low cost that was initially declared. A short timeline does not mean that the project won't last double that time. It is necessary to meticulously verify the product, the purchased system, and the vendor's readiness to execute the project. Extending the purchasing process and carrying out an initial analysis may require some extra time. Unfortunately, it will probably turn out that the client's requirements will result in more work, extended scope, and a longer timeline. The expectations can be reduced depending on the budget. However, these facts need to be transparently expressed, communicated, and included in the contract.

Sadly, reality needs to be embraced. If someone wants to buy a turn-key system or product that is objectively more expensive, they should be prepared for a higher cost and a longer timeline. It's necessary to foster an environment where suppliers are more professionally evaluated, and none of them are forced to include unrealistic prices or timelines in their proposals. The procurement process should not be a reverse auction.

Generally speaking, the price and timeline should not be the key criteria in the procurement process. The goal should be to assess the offer in terms of objectives and business outcomes. The product or system should undergo thorough verification of the vendor's readiness, actual costs, and project timeline.

Why It Doesn't Make Sense

All of the preceding practices are described in regard to the contradicting interests of particular actors or the parties involved in the sales process and the dishonest behavior in the purchasing processes leading to creating "impossible" projects. But it makes absolutely no sense. People try to achieve their particular goals and benefits. Clients and vendors play very well-known games—the clients demand impossible things, and vendors agree to those terms.

Regardless of what is put in the contract, the workload in the project is, to some extent, objective. Projects last as long as they need to last. So what's the point of putting in the contract an unrealistic timeline and then running the project in a war mode, constantly arguing with the client, making excuses, and forcing people to work in conditions leading to burnout? The project will probably take as long as the experts assume. What's the point of distorting reality and promising that the product is complete when it's not, or just hoping that things will sort out by themselves? One thing that is certain is that the overly optimistic scenario won't come true, and the project will cost more and last longer.

As an example, let's take a project for a large corporation from Western Europe, a formerly state-owned business with tens of thousands of employees and mature purchasing processes. Developing and implementing the product took more or less three times longer than initially planned. The development of extra features took some more years. It could have been anticipated from the start. But both parties had some illusions about it. The "expected" budget was approved. And all this happened with the mature purchasing processes in place in one of the largest companies in Western Europe. It's a shame that it had nothing to do with reality. Sadly, similar stories keep happening.

If a project is executed openly, honestly, and transparently from the beginning, both parties focus on facts and consistently deliver. They don't argue. They don't fight over the scope, delays, or deliverables on both sides. Such conflicts only lead to delays. In practice, by signing the contract on unrealistic terms, you cause the project to last as long as it should last and cost as much as it should anyway, but on top of that, you waste time managing conflicts, arguments, blame games, scope disputes, and so forth.

It's the projects that run openly and honestly that more often succeed, are cheaper, and end sooner. It's another reason why agile methods and time and material approaches are more effective.

It's necessary to eliminate dishonest practices in sales and procurement processes. It's a complex issue as it refers to changes in corporate management systems and organizational processes, including reward and compensation systems.

CHAPTER 4

Can an Impossible Project Be Completed?

When something is important enough, you do it even if the odds are not in your favor.

—Elon Musk

In the previous chapters, you learned what impossible projects are and why and how they are even created in the first place. Next, it makes sense to ask whether such projects can be effectively delivered and what this means exactly. In theory, an impossible project is bound to fail immediately. After all, we're dealing with large-scale problems, recurring delays, expanding ("exploding") scope, financial losses, an incompetent team, a lack of subject matter expertise within the company, a vague or constantly changing project goal, an unfriendly or even hostile attitude on the client's side, constant pressure to deliver "more and better" (regardless of the project scope), lack of decision-making or surprising, destructive and unpredictable client's decisions, often leading to penalty charges or even terminating the contract by the client.

© Marcin Dąbrowski 2025
M. Dąbrowski, *10 Rules for Impossible Projects,*
https://doi.org/10.1007/979-8-8688-1463-1_4

The problems listed can occur in various combinations. So, if it's clear that the delivery will be delayed, or the project cannot be completed on time or according to the contract, or that the project will generate losses, and so on, what's the point of continuing or even starting the project? Well, as it turns out, there are examples of projects that, taking all criteria into account, should be considered impossible, were delivered to the client's satisfaction. This chapter looks at such projects and why they were ultimately delivered. You learn what success means for the client and why this definition may differ from the one constantly reminded by project management theory.

Examples of Impossible Projects That Were Successfully Delivered

Let's start with several examples of impossible projects that were bound to fail quickly. There was no chance of delivering the required scope on time and in quality in these projects, but despite all this, they were successfully delivered!

The goal of the first one was to carry out a complex business transformation in a company in Western Europe, where the vendor was supposed to replace the entire IT tool stack, which meant replacing over twenty different IT systems with a state-of-the-art platform, and then to take over its maintenance in a managed services model.

So, on one hand, it was an IT project of high complexity. On the other hand, it was necessary to design new business processes at the client's company. Yet another thing was that, as a result, the IT department would be reduced from 50 people working on the old systems to only a few whose job would be to oversee the quality of services offered by the new IT platform. The project could be qualified as impossible from the start.

First, the vendor had to develop the IT platform from scratch, but the timeline was as if all the components had already existed! Second, it was a new business domain that the vendor had only started investing in. Thus, no experts or specialists had yet to be recruited. Third, the project's goal contradicted the goals of the users and the IT department staff! Finally, it was necessary to collaborate with ten-odd subcontractors (mainly hardware and technology providers), each of which was resistant as all of them had competitive IT systems, and the built platform was supposed to introduce control mechanisms to monitor the quality of their work.

Despite all this, the project was a success. What contributed to that? Both the client and the vendor had a positive attitude. The top executives were personally committed to the project to the extent that the project manager on the vendor side had direct access to the management both on the vendor and on the client side! Each problem was solved immediately and in a constructive way.

The vendor had problems developing the platform on time as the system was developed practically from scratch while acquiring domain knowledge, organizing the team (which grew from 10 to 200 people), and aligning the requirements with several various groups of interests. Indeed, there were delays, pressure, and difficult discussions with the client.

Admittedly, however, the vendor's team was unusually motivated, proactively dealing with all the problems head-on. Even when the client was facing challenges, the vendor was always pragmatically helping. The client felt that the vendor was doing their best for the project to finish successfully—the client understood that despite delays and issues, there was no alternative on the market.

The current vendor displayed an attitude of partnership and pragmatism. Even though the project was delayed by three years, the delivered scope significantly differed from the planned scope. The client organization achieved its business goals (which also evolved along the way) and was very satisfied with the outcomes. The client willingly recommended the vendor for the following couple of years.

Another example is about a transformation of similar complexity, but this time, the project was set in one of the countries of central Europe. The goal here was also to replace an outdated environment of legacy IT systems with a state-of-the-art platform, which (as you can imagine) only existed on paper in the vendor's offer. Both parties, meaning the client and the vendor, generally agreed to the project's key objectives, some high-level expectations and scope, and the timeline of deliveries. On this basis, the vendor offered a price that was significantly lowered during the sales and negotiation process. As a result, an impossible project was initiated.

The contracted schedule was planned to deliver a ready-made product, but the "product" did not exist and had to be developed from scratch. To do that, some domain knowledge was necessary. However, like in the previous case, this time, it was uncharted territory for the vendor organization, and they had neither the expertise nor the team.

To make matters worse, the simplified objectives for the project, which had been agreed with the client, came to nothing as soon as the prospective users expressed their opinions. Apparently, they had no idea what had been decided as the talks were only between the management representatives. But they had their own expectations, which consisted of (as it happens) transferring the features of the old legacy systems into the new platform so that their everyday tasks would remain unchanged. As you can imagine, the revenue planned in the contract was not enough to cover the costs. As a result, the project generated losses and was not treated as a priority by the vendor's organization. On the contrary, the managers avoided involving their people at all costs.

As a consequence, the project lacked resources and competencies. The work was severely delayed. The client's and vendor's teams fought at every step of the process to prove themselves right about the scope. On the vendor side, the management team put pressure on completing the project, but they wanted it to be profitable while also taking people away from other projects. Despite several years of delay, the project was finally finished. The client obtained the expected platform. The vendor developed a new product that could be sold to other clients. Moreover, thanks to the client's referral, the vendor got other contracts from sister companies belonging to the same group in other countries. It shows that a project doomed to fail according to any management theory was delivered and generated a lot of benefits for both parties.

The last example concerns an IT system implementation in a large company in Western Europe. The vendor offered a product that was partially non-existent. Both the client and the vendor made some overly optimistic assumptions at the offering stage, which proved wrong when the users had their say. The reality turned out to be much more complex. After completing one of the phases, the migration and data cleaning took as long as a year!

To make matters worse, the vendor offered a price that was too low, mostly to hit their annual sales targets. The project generated such a high loss that after two years, the vendor suspended the project after completing the first of three phases. Despite that, from the client's point of view, the project was successful to a large extent. Why was that? Even though there were some issues, it was clear to the client that the vendor organization did their best, that they tried to solve problems, proactively looked for solutions, and that there was some understanding of the client's business and organizational processes on the client's side. It was obvious that any other vendor would have faced similar challenges. The client also understood the financial problems, but there was no budget for delivering extra scope. That's why the project was suspended. Only the first part of the system was released to production, and the client was satisfied. After some time, the client was taken over by a larger company, a new budget was assigned, and the project was restarted.

These examples have one thing in common: they were delayed by several years. The scope of these projects kept changing or was eventually much larger than stated in the contract. What's more, the business goals also evolved. The client commissioned one thing, got another, yet somehow considered the project successful.

The management of both parties wanted to see the project complete, and they also saw the value of a long-term relationship. The vendors developed new products and received valuable referrals. The clients had no alternative and knew that despite the challenges, nobody else could complete the project and that, despite some tensions, it was important for the vendor to deliver the project. Any other company would face similar issues.

The problems presented by the projects were not a result of inappropriate project management methodology or mistakes in implementation. They were a consequence of some other harmful patterns which are the subject of this book.

The Client's Definition of a Successful Project

To understand why an impossible project can be delivered, it is important to consider the client's definition of a successful project. It's not always delivering the scope in the expected quality and on time. When it comes to large transformations, it's only theory. The client's perception and the project's success are not always aligned with the project management principles. Such projects usually last several years. At this time, the goals and clients' expectations have evolved. Even the client's vision of what they want to achieve, what they need, and why they need it changes over time. It is often said, "We start one project and deliver a completely different one."

This is best shown by the example of a complex IT project carried out by a large company in Western Europe. When the contract was signed, it was planned to use a big bang approach, meaning that all of the functional areas of the new platform would be launched at once, and all the legacy systems would be replaced at once, too. Eventually, for many different reasons, the areas were implemented sequentially, one by one.

According to the contract, the project was supposed to be completed within two years. In reality, it took five. The project started with one group of suppliers of the technology the system was specified for. But, it was finished with a completely different one, which affected the scope, the timeline, and the budget. Interestingly, the project was successful from the client's perspective, even though the scope differed from what was planned. The contract was 1000 pages long, so one could assume that it should be quite specific and well-defined.

So, how can you even talk about the success of such a project from the management theory point of view? Why was the client satisfied and considered the project a successful undertaking? Why did the client see the vendor as a partner and want to continue working together? It did not deliver the scope per the contract, and the work was completed on time and within budget! It turns out that the clients care more about the proactive approach, engagement, partnership, understanding their situation, a long-term relationship, trust, and so forth.

In transformational projects, goals often change, and clients expect flexibility from vendors, both in terms of the scope and the timeline. Clients value a proactive approach, pragmatism, and meeting their expectations. They don't want arguments about each deviation from the contract terms. They expect the vendor to be present, available, and open for conversations; they want to be listened to.

Clients want vendors to understand their organization and their specific challenges. The client will always choose a vendor who understands them, is responsive, and is willing to help even in case of problems and delays in the project. Clients prefer a partner who's always there to help over an arrogant vendor who points out mistakes and supposedly delivers the scope as stated in the contract.

That's why the definition of a successful project is quite vague. The longer the project, the more complex it gets, and the more the success criteria differ from the ones defined before the vendor selection process even started! Then, the quality of the partnership becomes even more important.

In a nutshell, you could say that the key to a successful project is a partnership, a proactive approach, and showing understanding for the client, especially when it comes to impossible projects. They are delayed anyway. Their scope fluctuates and changes. Even the client's expectations change. The business environment changes. However, the clients still value partnerships and a proactive approach.

10 Rules for Delivering Impossible Projects

As you saw in the examples, impossible projects can be delivered! If possible, a set of rules must significantly increase the chances of success. If you apply them, you demonstrate your proactive approach to the client, understand their circumstances and challenges, and display partnership. You will run the project pragmatically and effectively, but it is often achieved by contradicting popular opinions, against management theory, and against human or organizational instincts. Last but not least, you will ensure that the project makes business sense for your organization and that the impossible project is not stopped by the client or the management of your organization.

Of course, more rules can be formulated. This book is not academic but a practical guide for navigating the business environment. I have described the 10 most important rules that help any project manager succeed. These rules allow project managers to be more effective and deliver difficult projects!

10 Rules for Delivering Impossible Projects

Rule 1: Get involved in the contract negotiation.

Rule 2: Define what it means to "deliver" the project.

Rule 3: Be helpful and show commitment.

Rule 4: Build relationships and the power of influence.

Rule 5: Focus on progress and be pragmatic.

Rule 6: Exert pressure and use your position.

Rule 7: Consciously manage information flow.

Rule 8: Take care of the project's financial condition.

Rule 9: Create and document your project history.

Rule 10: Focus on the long-term relationship with the client.

These rules always work! They save projects that could be stopped despite the good results and being run properly in every aspect. They dramatically increase the chances of delivering projects that, at first glance, are deemed to fail. These rules are independent of and complementary to the project management methods.

The next part of this book explains why specific project management methods don't solve the problems of impossible projects. Then, it moves on to discussing the 10 rules in more detail.

PART II

Methodologies and Certifications: BS

CHAPTER 5

Certificate Factory

In theory, there is no difference between theory and practice. But in practice, there is.

—Lawrence Peter Berra

Project management methodologies have their advantages and address several important issues. They put a frame on the knowledge and the entire project management area. They provide descriptions of particular techniques, present various ways of running a project, pinpoint the things that should be taken into consideration, and so forth. And thus, they are quite beneficial. These are, however, just some basic tools, a skillset that should get you started. They are neither a guarantee of success nor are they a solution to some real-life problems. Methodologies are a good way of organizing knowledge. They identify the areas that should be managed. These include the scope, change, timeline, quality, budget, and stakeholders. Project management methodologies don't tell you exactly how to do it, what kind of problems you will encounter, or how to solve them.

Project management methodologies provide a partial description of tools and techniques: where and how to keep the information about the scope of the project, how to record changes, how to construct a schedule, how to estimate the costs, and the deviations from the scope and timeline. But we are still dealing with the basics and the necessary skill set. Knowing where and how to document the scope and the changes does not mean we know how to manage the scope with the client, which is the key part. It's not hard to record some clear elements of the scope in any project management tool according to any given methodology. The challenge is to discuss with the client how certain requirements translate into a specific scope of work. In the same vein, documenting the schedule in Microsoft Project or any other tool is simple. It's hard to agree on it with the team and ensure that the estimates are accurate. Someone could say that applying agile methods and T-shirt sizing of tasks solves the problem. Absolutely not. There's still uncertainty, but we simply admit it. We're just being more transparent about it. According to project management methodologies, you need to take care of quality. And how does it help the company that you're currently working for? Some processes address the quality issue. You need to build a team, but how to do it exactly? You need to take care of the budget. It's hardly a challenge to record project costs and report them. Anyone could do it even without any methodology. It's hard to manage the work so that it's cost-effective. It's hard to persuade the client to pay for the scope creep. It's extremely hard to run a project that was wrongly priced and generates a loss. No methodology can help you in doing that!

Certifications vs. Practice and Experience

Completing a project management course, regardless of the methodology, does not mean that you know how to manage projects—just like learning the alphabet does not turn you into a poet or novelist. Obtaining a certification in any given methodology only means that you can answer test questions, which will let you pass the certification test.

Let's take a closer look at the process of preparing for the examination that leads to obtaining the certificate. Some courses focus on teaching how to answer specific test questions. There are a lot of coursebooks that present the methodology but also put a lot of emphasis on teaching how to answer specific test questions. I also studied from those coursebooks many years ago when I took my PMP exam. At that time, I had very limited experience managing several R&D projects with a team of 10 people. Those projects were internal, and we didn't have to interact with the client. Of course, I got my PMP certification. And what changed in my project management experience and skill set? Nothing! It only helped me to upgrade my resume. It did not provide me with any practical knowledge. It was the same with the Prince2 Practitioner certificate and many others.

I gained experience only by working with real clients and real teams within real organizations. They were the best teachers! Working with people and clients, overcoming obstacles, and looking for pragmatic solutions to real problems made me a seasoned project manager. For instance, anyone with the PMP certification knows that if some requirements are outside the agreed scope, you need to initiate a change procedure. Fantastic! How simple is that! As boxers say, everybody has a game plan until they get punched in the mouth. According to the methodology, you inform the client that we need to initiate the change procedure because of the requirements that (in our view) extend the scope of work. The client replied that, in their opinion, the work was within the scope and refused to start the procedure. Then, a seasoned project management practitioner presents a range of pragmatic solutions that have nothing to do with any methodology and are not a part of any exam. They are often solutions and techniques that are not openly talked about!

Certification should be treated as a confirmation of course completion in a particular project management methodology. The knowledge is definitely useful. It enhances the skillset. It widens the horizons. It makes it easier to align the approach to the situation at hand. It makes it easier to communicate with the client in terms of mutual expectations toward managing the project.

However, we can't put an equation mark between having certifications and practical skills, experience, and the ability to manage projects. These are two very different things!

Certificate Factory

Why are certifications so popular, then? Why are we bombarded with ads urging us to obtain them?

First and foremost, project management methodologies are a big business! Especially in the area of training! There are companies selling coursebooks, study materials, and running courses focused on preparing for a specific exam. Authors specialize in writing these coursebooks. There are associations for "evangelists" of a particular methodology.

There are also trainers and consultants who promise that your company will flourish after implementing one or another project management approach. It's interesting how these people often come with ready recipes and answers. They assume up front that they know the problem and its solution. Then it turns out that you paid someone to come to your organization, put some check marks on the checklist or template, get a lot of insider information (to use in subsequent training assignments), and create negligible outcomes. The reason is very simple. As I mentioned multiple times, project management methodologies are not a recipe for fundamental problems for IT companies. They do not provide a simple recipe for project success; neither are they a cause of its failure.

Interestingly, from the organization's point of view, the training business does not take any accountability for delivering valuable outcomes. Its goal is to sell as many training materials, courses, and exam tokens as possible. Each business has its own marketing strategy. In this case, it's persuading potential customers that obtaining this or that certificate will turn them into professionals and earn them any employer's respect, and all their projects will succeed. Then, clients and business reality mercilessly verify it.

An even more interesting aspect of this business is making new versions of known methodologies and frameworks to put pressure on the need to get new certificates. You pass an exam, and two or three years later, you need to renew your certificate because there is a new version of the methodology. You can wonder what groundbreaking changes have been introduced over this short period of time if projects are still delayed. Some certificates expire or must be upgraded, which generates new business, such as earning points.

In all this madness, it's easy to forget that studying and subsequently implementing the known and most popular project management methodologies is not an obligation. It's an artificially generated pressure. The most commonly applied methods might not be optimal for your company. We tend to forget that many of these methods or approaches were created based on the working methods used in specific companies or organizations. Then, for various reasons, they were popularized, either due to these organizations' deliberate actions or thanks to the commercial success of a given organization (e.g., Spotify).

Your Project Management Approach: Common Sense and Drawing on the Company History

Applying and implementing project management methodologies blindly because they are popular is a mistake. Someone heard that this is how to manage projects, and we want to keep up. People expect magical solutions in the following vein: "We implement method X, and suddenly, all our projects will be profitable and delivered on time." It's not surprising, considering that we're constantly bombarded with information, articles, books, and ads, which assure us that it will surely happen. Then some consultants are hired, but the truth is that they spend most of their time being instructed and filled with information from the people from our own company! We are the ones providing knowledge about how the company operates and what its business characteristics are. Then, it turns out that the project management method they specialize in is perfect for our business. The question is who should pay whom and for what? It can often seem that the consultant gains more than the company implementing the proposed methodology.

First, you need to conduct a thorough analysis, diagnose the causes of the problems, and then select and implement the right project management methodology. For example, if the root of the problem is that at the sales stage, the company failed to ensure that the project can be delivered with the available resources, no methodology or approach will solve the issue. If the offers that the company sends out do not contain a detailed description of the product's features, then regardless of how effectively we manage the scope, it is bound to expand because the contract will not be specific enough. And so on.

The methods you choose for managing your project should depend on its specific context: the industry, the product or system that is to be delivered, your production system constraints, availability of resources, competencies that are currently available, and the ones that need to be acquired, the team's experience, including the leaders of specific areas and the project manager himself. While selecting the methodology, you should consider the company's experience and history of past projects, successes, and failures, as well as the factors contributing to successes and leading to failures.

And finally, you need to consider the client's organization and its characteristics. What are the expectations, what project management approach do they prefer, how does the organization operate, which ways of working are most effective, and which should be avoided? It's quite clear that analyzing all these aspects while selecting the appropriate project management methodology is not an easy task. Therefore, it's rather unlikely that you will find a perfectly suited project management methodology that can be just taken off the shelf, and it's unrealistic to assume that the project is bound to succeed thanks to any specific approach. Unfortunately, it doesn't work like that. There are always trade-offs.

For this reason, companies often develop their own methods and processes that are optimal for their specific context. These methods are not usually known, but there are some exceptions, like Spotify's example. Many known project management methodologies started as approaches created and used in specific companies and were only later publicized. Some of these "homemade" methods evolved into renowned standards. A good example is PRINCE2, which was created based on the PROMPT methodology first applied by Simpact Systems. It should be an incentive to create your own project management approach. The concepts that are right for the particular context and situation. Knowing other project management methodologies helps you create your own. It may inspire you to come up with even better ideas.

To Sum Up

This chapter examined the lack of correlation between the project management certification and practical skills and experience in this area. We also talked about who and why creates the pressure to obtain certificates. We touched upon a very important aspect of creating popular project management methodologies, which are largely a result of some companies' experiments. These companies were bold enough to create practical approaches on their own instead of applying what was available. Finally, their methods were made available to the wider public.

The next chapter looks at why project management methodologies are useless when facing the key challenges of impossible projects.

CHAPTER 6

The Uselessness of Methodologies and Certificates in the Face of Key Problems of Impossible Projects

The death knell for any enterprise is to glorify the past—no matter how good it was.

—Jeff Bezos

Project management methodologies are good as a basic skill set that any project manager should have. They should be seen as a foundational knowledge base to build upon. They give you a vocabulary set and some necessary tools and techniques. Methodologies are often a form of a checklist, both in terms of areas to manage and tasks that should be taken into account.

© Marcin Dąbrowski 2025
M. Dąbrowski, *10 Rules for Impossible Projects*,
https://doi.org/10.1007/979-8-8688-1463-1_6

But, project management methodologies have one major flaw. They do not help solve key problems! These are the problems that are most often encountered at the intersection of business and the relationship with your customer. However, you don't need any methodology to solve technical problems!

What's more, an impossible project doesn't become successful just because you decided to apply one or another project management methodology. It's not about the choice of a particular methodology nor about abiding by its principles. Success depends mostly on the client's definition and interpretation of success. It has nothing to do with any project management methodology, whether modern or popular.

This chapter focuses on proving the uselessness of project management methodologies in the face of key problems encountered in impossible projects. As a reminder, these problems are as follows.

- Persistent and recurring delays

- Expanding or "exploding" scope

- Financial losses

- Lacking resources, no team

- Insufficient domain knowledge in the company

- Undefined or constantly changing project goal

- Unfavorable or even hostile attitude on the client's side

- Constant client's pressure to deliver more and better (regardless of the project's scope)

- Clients avoiding decisions

- Astonishing destructive or unpredictable decisions or actions on the client's side

- Penalty charges threats to put the project on hold or to terminate the contract

The following sections take a closer look at each of these problems and the reasons why project management methodologies do not help solve them.

Recurring Delays

In general, delays can be divided into "sold" delays and those occurring during the project. The former type happens before the project is initiated, as early as the sales process. At this stage, an unrealistic timeline is agreed upon, while it's clear that sticking to it is just objectively impossible for several reasons. When the contract is signed, the vendor commits to completing the scope of work by the deadline that is impossible to meet.

Recurring delays are most often linked to this type of delay. The team will never be able to make up for lost time. It's simply impossible as more time is needed to complete the agreed scope of work. However, from the client's perspective, there seem to be recurring delays in the project. This is the kind of problem that no methodology can solve. And the reason for that is simple. Any project management method helps you to work more effectively, but they are not designed to solve business problems, especially those related to a project with unrealistic contract terms. Solutions to this type of problem are a part of client relations management. They involve proper communication strategies and the right approach to the client.

On the other side of the spectrum, recurring delays occur after the project has started. In this case, delays result from objective technical or organizational challenges. Technical issues are usually solved by spending enough time on discussions among experts. It works the same way every time, regardless of the project management approach. The organizational aspects may refer to various areas. They are usually related to the operational characteristics of the company, both on the vendor and client side. No matter your project management approach, you need to adapt to this specific context anyway.

To solve organizational problems, you need to delve into the operational aspects of a given company (clients, vendors, or partners). There are some classical examples. Let's assume that you apply agile methods. From the vendor's point of view, delays are often a result of a lack of or unavailability of business analysts on the client's side, which causes issues with defining the scope on time.

Another problem resulting in a prolonged delivery time is a too general scope and extensive discussions with the client about what should actually be done. Yet another problem is not following their own estimates by the team. The ability to estimate individual tasks by individual people is also unrelated to any project management approach but to the product itself, the system, technology, industry, or the individual's experience. You could say that in agile, you use T-shirt sizing, and velocity is measured transparently. It is the case, of course.

In other words, this approach proposes that we admit openly to the client that the estimates are inaccurate, that we don't know exactly when the scope will be delivered, and that the accuracy of the timeline will be known in retrospect. Does it solve the problem of open communication and admitting to uncertainty? It does. Does it solve the delay problem? No.

Even the most modern and popular project management approach does not solve the problem of recurring delays when dealing with impossible projects!

Expanding or "Exploding" Scope

One of the most insidious problems encountered in impossible projects is an improperly or too generally described scope of work. The initial enthusiasm for signing the new contract obscures the reality. We're embarking on a new, exciting journey. We're getting to know the client. We're calculating the future profits. Gradually, it turns out that the scope of work expanded, that it was larger than we thought, that the client may have failed to accurately describe their expectations, and that the project would cost more and last much longer.

If your problem is an improperly or too generally described scope, no project management methodology can change the estimates put in the contract! Admittedly, with some approaches, the truth will be exposed sooner or later in others. But if both parties signed the contract, it turns out that the reality expectations are much higher, the client is unwilling to make any concessions, and no methodology will give you a recipe for solving this issue. However, it must be pointed out that agile methods increase transparency, make communication more effective, and help in clarifying requirements. They don't solve the problem of inaccurate estimates, though.

The answers lie outside the methods. The possible courses of action refer both to client relations and the right attitude. They use a pragmatic approach to project management. The range of reactions is wide and depends on the client's attitude and the vendor's position resulting from the signed contract. For instance, you can discuss the situation with the client early on and solve the problem quickly. Of course, you need a partnership and an open-minded approach on both sides. You can also get into a conflict with the client, assign experienced, assertive business analysts, and negotiate the scope on the technical level, trying to persuade the client to accept your interpretation of the scope. You can adopt a confrontational approach, get on a warpath, and deliver the work according to your point of view. The management may try to renegotiate the contract. But these are not simple, enjoyable, or desirable solutions. Sometimes, however, you can choose either this way or generate losses and risk terminating the project.

But there is no situation when the solution to the expanding or "exploding" scope is a project management methodology!

Financial Losses

Generating financial losses on a project is a serious problem for the
finance director, the project team, and the client! If the vendor has no
adequate financing for the incurred costs, they usually act cautiously. It is
similar when the payment schedule is constructed so that the client does
not make any payments until the project is finished.

In the worst-case scenario, the project can generate constant financial
losses and be nothing but a liability for the vendor's business. Then, the
vendor also acts with caution. They don't want to take any risks. The
best people are assigned to more lucrative projects. They act cautiously
and in a reserved way. For obvious reasons, incurring costs for a project
that generates losses is risky. Consequently, the project is no longer the
vendor's priority, regardless of what they say in official meetings. The
project team has no resources, access to people, knowledge, or money.
Projects like this are very difficult. They generate a lot of stress and internal
and external conflicts. They lead to burnout on both sides.

The most common cause of financial losses in projects is signing
unprofitable contracts. It's not the project teams' fault or the incompetence
of the project managers! The root cause of the problem is the common
approach to the purchasing process on the client's side and the sales
process on the vendor's side. Both parties act in ways that negatively
impact the subsequent delivery of the project. Clients try to pressure
vendors to demand lower prices and faster delivery. Yet, for several
reasons, the vendors agree to these unrealistic terms. The matter is
complex and was discussed in my previous book, *Managing IT Projects*.

If the core of the issue here is that the contract price is too low in
relation to the cost of delivering the work, no project management
methodology can help! You can choose any of them; the result remains the
same! Project management methodologies do not help persuade the client
to pay more for the scope of work defined in the contract.

Lacking Resources/No Team

Another typical problem for impossible projects is the lack of resources in general, especially the lack of people in teams. When there are no necessary competencies or specialists on the team, and when the development team is too small to deliver the scope on time, meeting the project deadlines is impossible. If, for instance, to complete a certain phase of the project, you need three analysts, ten developers, and three testers, but you only have half of these specialists, then no matter whether you apply Agile, Scrum, PRINCE2, or any other approach or method, there's no way you can deliver the scope on time.

Project management methodologies do not solve the issue of lacking resources!

Of course, you could say that it's enough to assign the right people to the project, and the problem is solved. This is a perfect world scenario. When dealing with impossible projects, the resources are lacking for a reason. The situation is a mitigation strategy against further financial losses. Another reason might be that the company has different priorities with regard to invoicing or escalating and thus moves people to other, more important projects. There could also be a problem with finding the right people on the market. There can be various reasons for lacking resources. As per this discussion, the key thing is that implementing a project management approach cannot address the lack of resources. So, to deliver an impossible project, you need to focus on other measures.

No Domain Knowledge in the Company

Another typical problem for impossible projects is insufficient domain knowledge in the company that plans to develop a product or an IT system in an area that is still unchartered territory. It brings about various consequences. You don't understand the scope, so you don't understand the client's expectations. Therefore, effective communication is hard, and clearly describing the scope is impossible. The client is annoyed because the other party is not a partner in this conversation. The system creation is a painstaking process. The timeline keeps extending. The vendor can't test the system properly, and so on.

Like in the case of the previously described problems, you can apply whichever project management methodology you prefer, but the problem will remain unsolved! Competencies need to be built one way or another. You can acquire specialists from the market. You can enhance the team's skillset. You can hire a subcontractor or buy a company with the necessary competency, whether it's domain or technical knowledge.

Vague or Constantly Changing Project Goals

A very difficult problem to solve is a constantly changing business objective behind the project. In theory, there is a scope of work laid out in the contract. But, it usually refers to the business objectives defined by the client long before the purchasing process, which often goes back 6 to 12 months before signing the contract with the contractor! These objectives can already be different when the project starts, which—in the case of large projects—can happen 12 to 18 months after the decision about initiating the project.

The scope of work usually evolves throughout the project, and clients expect other features or applications of the features. There are changes in internal systems that your systems must be integrated with, and migration requirements will change as well. To make matters worse, the project timeline changes, and the sequence of the individual phases changes. The vendor was supposed to deliver a certain module first. But, when it's ready and submitted for testing, it turns out that it makes no sense for the users to try it without some extra modifications or changes or before delivering some other modules first. This is because business objectives

and the timeline of implementing changes in the business process on the
client's side change with time. Large transformation projects take years to
complete. Evolving business objectives, a lack of understanding of these
changes by the vendor, and a lack of adaptation and flexibility often lead to
conflicts at the top management level between the client and the vendor.

The vendor wants to work according to the terms of the contract, but
the client's situation is quite different from the one it was when signing the
contract. These problems and differences in the perception of the project
by the key persons on the client's side may lead to deterioration in the
vendor's reputation (even though the agreed scope is delivered on time) or
even to canceling the project or terminating the contract.

Project management methodologies give clear guidelines for what to
do when the client's expectations largely differ from what was put in the
contract. In this case, it is not about slight differences in the project's scope
but its complete redefinition. If you were to simply apply the principles
of project management methodologies, you'd submit a change request,
but where would you go with that? You'd have to inform the client that the
cost of the project has doubled as it has to be done virtually from scratch.
That would lead to the cancellation of the project and termination of the
contract. Adapting the project to the changing business context at the
client's company and the subsequent changes in their expectations is
not the kind of issue that you can address with any project management
methodology. The solution comes from applying 10 key principles
described later in this book.

Unfavorable or Hostile Attitude on the Client's Side

It's extremely hard to run a project when the client's attitude toward
your company is unfavorable or even hostile. This attitude can be
a systemic part of the project's environment. It happens when the

implemented system is seen as a threat by its future users as the aim of
its implementation may be to reduce staff or when the mother company
puts pressure on the management of the seemingly independent daughter
company to implement a solution against their will.

It also happens that a large group of people (or some key individuals)
on the client's side are just mean. They show off, emphasize their
superiority, try to prove that they're right, and offend the vendor's team.
These people can sabotage agreements or even entire meetings. It
indirectly impedes the analysis of the requirements, makes it difficult to
define tasks, and consequently leads to delays in the project and increases
its cost. It often causes problems with getting approvals for the modules
already delivered.

The hostile individuals who were supposed to approve some part of
the work with the users fail to do it, either deliberately or by negligence,
and then it turns out that some work has to be done again or modified.
These people may deflect reality, ruin the vendor's reputation, and
interpret the project metrics in such a way that it puts the vendor in a
negative light. As a result, the management on the client's side will be
inclined to withdraw from the cooperation and unlikely to increase the
volume of business done together; in case of more serious problems,
they might even charge penalty fees or cancel the project altogether. An
unfriendly attitude on the client's side also leads to burnout in the project
team. Nobody wants to work in an environment like this.

Project management methodologies do not help solve the problem
of an unfavorable or even hostile attitude on the client's side! However
professional and modern your approach is, it has no greater impact. The
client does not care. As mentioned, the solution to this problem is to use
the right approach on the vendor's side, skillfully managing the relations
with the client and key individuals, using your assets, and applying
pressure when necessary. All these solutions are described in the further
sections of this book, where you will find 10 rules for delivering impossible
projects.

The Client's Constant Demands for "More and Better"

Some clients can ruthlessly interpret the contract to their advantage in such a way that they get as much as possible. First, they exploit the fact that the scope of the project was described in general terms, leaving many details unspecified, which enables them to pressure the vendor to deliver more and more features. This, in turn, decreases the project's profitability, extends the timeline, and, in some extreme cases, leads to financial losses on the vendor's side.

Second, clients take advantage of unclear approval criteria definitions of delay or penalty mechanisms. If you as a vendor did not treat contract negotiations seriously enough in terms of protecting your own interests, in the course of the project, you can expect a prolonged approval process and some pressure on delivering new features without extra pay. You need to be aware that the client may threaten to charge penalty fees to get what they want.

There are regions of the world and clients where you have to fight to get your legitimate invoices paid. You deliver a milestone, the client formally approves it, you issue an invoice, and then you learn that the money will be transferred only after you have agreed to give an extra 100 man-days for features that the client wants for no extra pay. There are also clients who don't pay for the properly executed work but also demand that you continue working on the project.

Project management methodologies don't prescribe how to act when the client and the relationship with them fall into this category! You may choose any of them. You may inform the client that their demand is a change request. You may try to explain that according to the terms of the contract, they have to approve the work, that no penalty fee can be charged if the delay was the client's fault, that they have to pay the invoice, and so forth. And what if the client's answer is no? 10 rules of delivering impossible projects can help you in situations like that.

Clients Avoiding Decisions

One of the most common problems you will face when dealing with
difficult, impossible projects is the clients avoiding making a decision.
It usually concerns areas that are key for the vendor. Decision paralysis
leads to downtime, waiting, the inability to agree on key things, developing
features that are not approved, waste of time, delays, and cost increases.
Sometimes, decisions are delayed by the project team on the client's
side because they can't get the management's attention. Other times,
people hide the truth because they fear losing their jobs. Sometimes, the
client's management has some budget, administrative, legal, or political
constraints, and consequently, they avoid making decisions.

Also, in this case, project management methodologies are useless.
We're not dealing with issues resulting from how the client or the vendor
runs the project. It isn't about some critical mistakes, making the analysis
more effective, having a communications plan, cooperation, development
velocity, quality, and so forth. In this case, the client avoids making key
decisions that are necessary to continue the work effectively. The solution
here is to use the right methods of building pressure, using your bargaining
and legal position. You will find more on this in further sections of this
book, where you can find 10 rules for delivering impossible projects.

Astonishing, Destructive, and Unpredictable Decisions Made by the Client

One of the most dangerous situations that you will face while dealing
with difficult or impossible projects is illogical decisions made by the
client. They are often surprising or hard to understand, especially when
they negatively affect the project that the client should care about, at least
in theory. You may be running the project properly, applying the most
modern project management approach. Yet, all of a sudden, the client's

behavior becomes irrational. They, for example, cancel a large portion of
the scope, put the acceptance tests of the delivered software on hold, stop
the migration to the new system for no apparent reason, do not pay the
properly issued invoices, ask for adjusting the timeline of the project when
everything was going well, stops the communication or fails to respond,
takes on another vendor who does not change anything, and so forth.

These actions may seem irrational at first, but they are often a
consequence of some deliberate decisions made by the client, their
choices that were secretly made to apply a new strategy that will probably
be to your disadvantage, either because of canceling a large portion of the
scope, or because of a new timeline that is less advantageous in terms of
invoicing, or as a result of hiring a new vendor that plans to take over your
business. The reasons for that may be manifold.

Project management methodologies are based on some assumptions.
One of these assumptions is that the client's actions are rational and the
business environment is stable. They focus on working effectively in stable
conditions. However, they are not helpful when the client's behavior
becomes unreasonable. On the other hand, a situation like that does not
deem the project manager helpless, and there is the possibility to apply
countermeasures. There are some practical solutions that you can apply,
which are discussed later in this book.

Penalty Charges, Threats to Stop
the Project, or Contract Termination

When dealing with a difficult, wrongly estimated, impossible project,
naturally, you will face persistent delays. Unfortunately, it is an everyday
struggle. It needs to be pointed out again that it is an inherent feature of
improperly sold projects. The attempts at winning back the time are just
doomed to fail. It doesn't matter which project management methodology
you choose. The scale of the delay generated in the sales process is so

big that you can't speed up the work so much as to deliver the desired outcome on time. The problem here is not the inefficiency or poor performance but a wrongly estimated work and an unrealistic timeline decided during the sales process.

For obvious reasons, clients find it difficult to accept persistent delays. There's no point in wondering whether, in the sales process, they were aware that they were forcing potential vendors to commit to unrealistic schedules. When the project has started, and the contract has been signed, the client has the right to demand that the work is delivered according to the terms of the contract. When the client realizes that they are losing control of the pace of work and that there are no other ways to pressure the vendor, they can resort to threats of charging penalty fees. Expressing the intention is often enough. In some cases, though, clients do charge the penalty fees.

Nevertheless, each project, even the one that is run perfectly, can be canceled. There are plenty of examples of projects delivering the expected outcomes on time, where users were happy, yet the clients still canceled them.

Regardless of the project management methodology you choose, if the project is wrongly estimated, you will deal with recurring delays and threats of penalty charges. Also, no matter how well you run the project, the client can cancel it for several reasons, most often completely unrelated to whether the work is carried out according to the contract and the outcomes are as expected. Thus, as you can quite clearly see, project management methodologies neither protect you from the preceding problems nor tell you what to do when the client starts charging penalty fees or threatens to terminate the contract. However, 10 rules for delivering impossible projects can be helpful there.

To Sum Up

You need a theoretical foundation, experience, and practical knowledge to run projects effectively. Project management methodologies are a basic skill set that you should acquire. It needs to be kept in mind, though, that applying one or another project management approach has nothing to do with the project's success or failure. As you can see in this chapter, the majority of key problems you face in large and complex projects are not related to the methodologies you use and how well you abide by their principles.

CHAPTER 7

Practical Knowledge: The Missing Link

What we learn from history is that people don't learn from history.

—Warren Buffet

A good illustration of a brutal confrontation of theory with practice is a situation I experienced and will never forget. It was a project for a very big company. The contract was carefully crafted. The work was carried out according to the PMI methodology. The problem was that from the very beginning, the client insisted on getting many more features than were included in the project's scope. The project team took meticulous notes of all the potential scope creep. At the same time, the client was adamant about demanding the extra features yet unwilling to formally order the work, let alone pay for them. Moreover, the client insisted that the features be delivered according to a changed schedule. They wanted to add several intermediate stages of delivery that would require some additional testing, releasing, and acceptance phases. All this significantly delayed the delivery timeline, which the client blamed on the vendor.

I remember taking over this project at a critical moment. It had already been going on for two years. The client escalated the delays but wouldn't admit to extending the scope of work or changing the previously made

© Marcin Dąbrowski 2025
M. Dąbrowski, *10 Rules for Impossible Projects*,
https://doi.org/10.1007/979-8-8688-1463-1_7

agreements, which resulted in delays. A month after I took over the project, we went to the client's office to prepare the steering committee. While we were working on the presentation, the client insisted on extending the timeline by another year because they claimed that their team wouldn't be able to continue the work at the pace we proposed. Eventually, we concluded that it was their choice if the client wanted to extend the timeline.

The following day, however, during the first minutes of the steering committee and in the presence of the top management of both parties, the client informed us that the project was being canceled and the contract terminated. The reason they gave was the extra year of delay that they intentionally added. We were confused. The day before, the client's team insisted on adding the extra year.

I still vividly remember the situation. Even though the contract was carried out by the book, it was canceled, and to add insult to injury, it was done in a manner that left a lot to be desired and had nothing to do with business ethics. I can only assume that the client most probably ran out of budget for the project.

There are plenty of similar stories. Every time, they teach us a lesson. They show that theory is one thing, but real life and practical knowledge differ. Project management methodologies, certificates, and training courses are very useful. These are some theoretical foundations. However, they fail to prepare us to handle situations like the one described. To run difficult projects, you need practical experience, without which you will keep falling into the same traps. Practical knowledge lies in specific situations that the project managers dealt with, specific problems they faced, solutions they used, some behavioral patterns they applied, and so forth.

There are too few books on the market based on practical experience and showing how to cope with the most difficult issues. It might seem that each of these difficult situations is different and doesn't have a common denominator. However, it turns out that these situations fall into certain categories, and some patterns can be described. There are also some ways of dealing with them, and applying these solutions makes it much more likely that the project will be successfully delivered.

This book aims to identify the principles and practical solutions that should help you carry out projects pragmatically. These rules are as follows.

---

10 Rules for Delivering Impossible Projects

Rule 1: Get involved in the contract negotiations.

Rule 2: Define what it means to "deliver" the project.

Rule 3: Be helpful and show commitment.

Rule 4: Build relationships and the power of influence.

Rule 5: Focus on progress and be pragmatic.

Rule 6: Exert pressure and use your position.

Rule 7: Consciously manage information flow.

Rule 8: Take care of the project's financial condition.

Rule 9: Create and document your project history.

Rule 10: Focus on the long-term relationship with the client.

The upcoming sections of this book examine each of these rules in detail.

PART III

10 Rules for Delivering Impossible Projects

CHAPTER 8

Rule 1: Get Involved in the Contract Negotiations

The best way to predict the future is to create it.

—Peter Drucker

Contrary to what we're told during the training courses, what we read in most study books, and what is constantly repeated in the media, the biggest delays are not generated during the course of the project. It is very common during meetings with the client or with the management team of your own company to be blamed for the way the project is being managed. Each project manager has heard complaints about problems and delays. But it's necessary to point out one small but important detail. Delays and problems created during the project can usually be tracked down to some objective causes, which can be explained simply.

What's more, clients tend to understand and accept these explanations. It's different, though, when you need to explain why the project is delayed in relation to the agreed timeline (which, unfortunately for us, is a part of the contract) when on the vendor's side, it's clear that the project can't be delivered on time, that the product is largely incomplete

© Marcin Dąbrowski 2025
M. Dąbrowski, *10 Rules for Impossible Projects*,
https://doi.org/10.1007/979-8-8688-1463-1_8

or doesn't exist at all, that we lack domain knowledge, and in general the situation is quite different from the picture that was painted for the client during the quotation (offer preparation) process. At the sales stage, every aspect of the project is estimated and determined. Objectives are set, goals are discussed, the scope is defined, the timeline is drafted, acceptance conditions and penalty mechanisms are agreed upon, and so forth.

If inaccurate project parameters (regarding all aspects of the project) are agreed upon at the stage of signing the contract, it will be extremely difficult to deliver it and get back on track. A poorly negotiated contract is unlikely to be successfully delivered and won't be profitable.

A bad contract leads to a whole lot of problems regardless of the chosen project management methodology. An inappropriately sold project will never be successful or profitable, while a well-sold project can at least reach a break-even point. When dealing with this kind of project, you can expect delays, a dramatic increase in costs, escalations, conflicts, penalty charges, internal pressure exerted on the team, burnout, and high turnover.

If most of the key assumptions and—as a consequence—most of the project's problems are created during the sales process, how can you prevent that? The solution is simple. You need to get involved in the project during the offer preparation and contract negotiation stage! After the contract has been signed, it will be too late to change it. That's exactly why the first rule of delivering impossible projects is: "Get involved in the contract negotiations." In this way, you can largely influence the project itself, the environment you will be working in, and your chances for success.

The first thing to look at is whether the project's scope is defined in the contract and how it's defined. Is it described in detail and in a way that will make it clear what needs to be done? Or is it defined in very general terms? It is common that in the heat of the battle for a new client, the company tries to close negotiations as quickly as possible. As a consequence, the agreements that should be made and discussed with the client in more detail over a longer period of time are made hastily. It is usually the case that there is pressure to put simplified terms in the contract as there seems to be a high degree of understanding between the vendor and the client, and it's obvious what needs to be delivered.

Unfortunately, it doesn't work like that. If the scope is defined too generally, the project will likely be delayed and unprofitable. After signing the contract, for obvious reasons, the client will want to get more for less.

From an objective point of view, while conducting a detailed analysis of the solution, the vendor's assumptions about the workload will turn out to be largely underestimated with regard to the current demands of the client, who will say that this is exactly the system they were looking for and if something had been overlooked, it's the vendor's fault as "everything is stated in the contract."

Of course, the contract in question contains only some general terms, which leaves an open door for any interpretation of how a given functionality should behave. For instance, during the quotation process for one of the projects for a subsidiary of a large European group, many simplifications were made regarding how the work would be done.

The scope of the project was described in very general terms. After initiating the work on a new IT platform, which was supposed to be a product in itself, the client started insisting on copying features from various systems developed more than ten years before that had not been used until that time. Even though it was contradictory to the project's objectives, the scope of the project was not laid out clearly enough to prevent this kind of activity.

As a result, the vendor's costs doubled. The project was unprofitable and delayed from the start, and people were reluctant to work on it. Such sad stories can be avoided if you put effort into properly defining the scope of the project at the quotation (offer preparation) and negotiation stages.

It is at the sales stage that the scope is most "flexible." It is exactly the stage that can save you hundreds of thousands of man-days. Later, when the project has started, opportunities for introducing changes or optimizations will be very limited.

Thus, it is worth investing time in getting involved in the contract negotiations so that you can work on a project that is possible to be delivered, that has been realistically estimated, and where you can avoid misunderstandings related to the scope of work.

Likewise, it's the same with opportunities for some extra revenue. The offer preparation and negotiation stage gives you the biggest chance to define whether the project allows extra profit for paid extensions of the system—change requests (CRs). How the scope is defined determines whether it is possible to prove that some features are not in the scope. Even a very experienced team will be helpless if the contract is very general. The client will exploit the fact that the contract is vague, and they will claim that the features that seem an extension of the scope from the vendor's perspective are, in fact, a part of the project.

If you want to have an opportunity to get some extra paid assignments or some additional financing during the project, you need to make an effort and prepare for that at the quotation and sales stage.

Everything needs to be clearly stated in the contract. If you fail to do that, you will pay a high price during the course of the project. It's worth noting that, in most cases, projects are only a prelude to a long-term relationship with the client. After the defined scope of work has been completed, the most lucrative phase (from the vendor's point of view) begins, when the client keeps developing the system over the years based on the new requirements discovered during the project but also based on expectations resulting from the necessary adaptations to the changing business environment.

If the contract is very general and has a poorly defined scope, typically, the client will want to prepare for the future, so they will insist on developing features that will prepare the system for future demands from the implementation stage. That's why you need to ensure that the scope is very well described in the contract so that there are no doubts about it later. Projects are usually the least profitable stage of the relationship with the client. Therefore, you need to make sure that you can keep the costs under control during the project by preventing scope creep and unpaid work and also be able to generate extra revenue streams by selling extensions, such as the preceding CRs.

Furthermore, you can generate revenue after the project has been completed. In the following years, the client will keep having new needs. And they will pay only if necessary—if the contract says so. How to get there? When drafting and negotiating the contract, you need to make sure that after the first, most intensive part of the project is finished, the client will keep placing orders for new, extra-paid extensions. You just need to get involved in the quotation and negotiation process! It is very well illustrated in the example of a project delivered for a large European company. The system's basic features were delivered very late because (as is usually the case) the system that had been sold was largely non-existent. As a result, the first stage of the relationship with the client was unprofitable.

However, with time, it turned out that the client was planning to use the IT platform much more extensively. To do that, it was necessary to configure the system for extra devices that the system was controlling. The experienced analysts on the vendor's side had predicted this was still at the negotiation stage and ensured that the appropriate provisions were added to the contract. Thanks to that, the client kept ordering extra paid services to configure new devices, and the vendor could make up for the losses from the initial stages of the project!

If you want to make sure that the timeline of your future project is realistic, once again, you need to get involved already at the offer preparation and negotiation stage.

Generally speaking, delays can be divided into delays that had been "sold" with the project and those happening after the project started. The latter ones are a consequence of issues that arise during the project. Their causes are usually objective and understandable. They can be logically explained to the client. Then you can try to make up for lost time. Delays that are a problem are those that have been "sold" with the project or resulting from a timeline that is impossible to stick to for various reasons. They are usually connected with an unfortunate approach to the sales process by the client and the urge to sell at all costs on the vendor's side. So, the client insists on implementing the system in the shortest possible time and the vendor accepts the unrealistic expectations just to sign the contract.

The problem is that a timeline like this, unrealistic but included in the contract, is most often impossible to stick to. Delays generated in this way are a nightmare in projects and are significantly larger than those naturally arising during the project. An example bluntly showing the reality of the sold delay was a project in which, during the negotiations, the client insisted on shortening the time of one of the phases from three and a half years to one and a half years, which meant cutting the timeline by two years!

To win the deal, the vendor agreed to "optimize" the schedule. After half a year, it turned out that the phase in question would take two years, which was still one and a half years less than the development team estimated, but it would be delivered six months later than what was stated in the contract!

The key account manager (also responsible for signing the contract) wanted to know where the delay came from! Despite its ridiculousness, the situation shows that regardless of how unrealistic the plan would be, after signing the contract, both the client and the managers on the vendor's side will demand that the project milestones be delivered according to the contract!

That's why if you want to deliver the project on time, you need to ensure it is possible at the stage of submitting an offer and contract negotiation!

You need to get involved at this stage even though the project hasn't started formally. In contrast, there is a positive example where, at the quotation stage, the client and the vendor held a series of workshops over several weeks, as a result of which the client concluded that in light of the complexity and size of the scope, the project should take two years longer and that, because the expectations where not entirely clear, it felt that the work should be billed on a T&M (time and materials) basis. In this case, the client demonstrated experience and wisdom in correctly anticipating that including an unrealistic timeline into the contract and a fixed price, fixed scope formula for the work would have no chance of success and would only lead to conflict, escalation, and further delays.

If you want to ensure that the project has the right level of funding at all times, that your company treats it with the right priority and therefore provides you with the people and resources to carry out the tasks, and that your team works in good conditions, that people want to take part in your project, then an appropriate payment schedule is necessary.

Importantly, it must be handled at the contract negotiation stage! After that, it will be too late. The payment schedule (i.e., the distribution of the amounts you plan to invoice during the contract period) is a fundamental issue. Of course, when acquiring a new customer, the vendor's enthusiasm obscures the real picture. Vendors often accept a payment schedule in which most of the revenue is only invoiced when the work is completed, the result being that they then carry out the work on credit, with no financing and no guarantee of payment.

For clients, the situation is advantageous. After all, they can withdraw from the cooperation without incurring any major costs. This type of arrangement only leads to a passive and cautious attitude on the part of the vendor. If they aren't sure that the project will be successful and that the client won't cancel it, they will obviously not commit costs and won't willingly invest in an uncertain undertaking. The project, therefore, ends up at the bottom of the priority list. As a result, by applying an aggressive payment schedule with invoicing of larger amounts only after the project is completed, the client only causes a situation in which the project is run cautiously and gets delivered much later than if they had agreed to fund the work proportionately with the costs incurred. The issue of the payment schedule is very often overlooked. People overwhelmingly focus on the project scope and timeline; in other words, on whether it is even possible to deliver what the client expects on time. The problem is that the financing conditions of a project translate directly into the working environment of the team and the availability of people and resources.

Business unit managers, who have to deliver financial results year after year, will always direct people and resources to projects that provide revenue in a given year and allow them to meet their financial goals. Consequently, no matter what, if your project does not generate regular revenue, runs on credit, or does not allow the business unit managers to hit their targets, then you can expect to see people gradually disappear from your team, either because of other new projects or because of escalations with other clients (who pay fairly), and so forth. It's impossible to think about stable planning in such an environment. All of this can be avoided. You must get involved in negotiations and fight for a favorable payment schedule before the contract is signed! After that, it will be too late.

One of the typical concerns of a project manager is the threat of penalty charges for delays. This is hardly surprising. Penalty amounts can run into millions. They can significantly impact the finances of entire companies, cause conflicts between the client and the vendor, destroy relationships, or even close development opportunities, affecting the careers of individuals. Avoiding penalties in impossible projects (i.e., those that have either been badly sold or have become unrealistic for other objective reasons) is very difficult. It is impossible to overcome certain "laws of physics."

It goes without saying that you should try to deliver a project on time, but very often, this is objectively impossible.

The best way to avoid potential penalties is not to work nights or weekends or add a large number of people to a project until you end up disrupting its profitability. There is a better way, which is effective and quick but extremely difficult! You simply have to define sufficiently secure mechanisms for calculating penalties in the contract! In other words, you have to get involved in contract negotiations, and there, you have to fight for the right provisions even before the project starts!

The biggest problem is the vagueness of the provisions on the calculation of penalties. If you have agreed that they can be applied in any situation where a project is delayed, regardless of who is at fault, it will be difficult to defend your team later if the client decides to apply financial punishment.

There are usually three approaches to choose from here: penalties are charged if the project is delayed, if it is delayed and the vendor is to blame, or if it is delayed and the vendor is solely responsible. It is quite clear that the first case is the least favorable. For example, the client can delay approving the analysis document and run tardy integration tests, and as a result, the project is delayed, so penalties can be charged. The second case is better but also suboptimal.

You should always strive to ensure that penalties can only be applied for delays for which the vendor is solely responsible. That way, if the client wants to penalize your team for delaying the project in the future, and you can show that work on the client's side contributed to the delay, you can (in theory) argue that your team is not the one to take full responsibility.

However obvious it may sound, ensuring that these provisions are in the contract is crucial, and it will largely influence both the health of the project and how the potential conflicts with the client are handled. For example, in one of the projects, the contract contained a clause about penalty charges in case of delays, regardless of who was at fault. After some time, the client started to exploit these clauses. The project was indeed delayed. It turned out to be more complex than previously assumed. Both sides generated the delays.

On the other hand, the client cleverly exploited the situation and, by constantly threatening to charge penalty fees, forced concessions from the vendor and demanded extra features (in exchange for waiving penalties). If it had been stipulated in the contract that penalties could be applied in the case of delays caused by the sole fault of the vendor, this situation would not have taken place! Therefore, to protect the project from potential penalties, the best way is to get involved in negotiations and ensure that the appropriate contractual provisions are in place.

After the delivery of the complete IT system or a part of it, there comes the time for acceptance tests. Every member of the project team intuitively feels that if the system meets the customer's expectations, its performance is satisfactory, and it contains no serious defects, it should be formally approved. And this is where our intuition and common sense are often confronted with harsh reality.

There are projects where the acceptance criteria are described in very general terms. There are no specific, numerically quantified parameters, such as no critical class errors, five major class errors, and any number of minor class defects. In one project for a large institution, it was generally stated in the contract that each stage of the project would be approved upon successful completion of acceptance tests. No specific levels of quality were specified.

As a result, the approval process for this project took months, while the standard is two or three weeks! The vendor was forced to fix many insignificant cosmetic defects, some of which were also due to oversights on the client's part. The system's overall quality was exquisite; the project was delayed by several months, and the vendor's costs were much larger than previously planned.

In another project, where the acceptance criteria were very well defined in the contract, the client, together with representatives of the business departments, cooperated on the evaluation and classification of the errors, assessing which ones needed to be fixed, by when, what their impact on the business operation was, which ones were critical, which ones were only a nuisance, and which ones could be fixed at a later date. In this project, the approval process was carried out efficiently. Even the client was very satisfied because the system could be implemented faster. They were able to boast about the success of the project within the organization and introduce new users more quickly, which considerably sped up the adoption of the new tool.

Acceptance criteria and approval conditions are not minor issues. Depending on the client, they can make your life unpleasant, generate overheads, and severely delay the project. This is why you need to be involved in the negotiations and personally ensure that the relevant contractual provisions are included.

Finally, once the project is completed, we usually move on to the maintenance phase of the system. It is also crucial to know how the expected quality parameters are defined, how they are calculated, and with what effort the vendor can fulfill them. The way penalties are calculated for failing to meet the expected SLA level is also very important: whether the calculation mechanism is fair, not too restrictive, and whether the total penalties in a given settlement period are limited.

There are draconian contracts in which the client can charge penalties higher than the vendor's remuneration for a given system maintenance period, making the provision of SLA services largely unprofitable. There are also contracts in which vendors are so clever in designing the mechanism for calculating penalties that even a very low level of service does not translate into a noticeable loss of revenue—vendors have no incentive to care about the level of quality. In contrast, clients have no tools to do anything about it.

From a project management point of view, it is important to get involved already at the negotiation stage and define the SLA parameters for the maintenance period together with the sales team.

In addition to the previously mentioned mechanism for calculating penalties, it is also necessary to define precisely which incidents will be treated as violations and which can occur without affecting the reported quality of the delivered service. At all costs, we must avoid a situation where any type of incident can be interpreted as a critical fault. Unfortunately, there are contracts in which, according to the negotiated terms, the "occurrence of critical errors" for, say, two months in a row can be grounds for contract termination but which (at the same time) lack a precise definition of what this "critical error" really means and do not specify how many such incidents must occur to violate the agreement! We must avoid the lack of precision in the contract at all costs.

Once again, it is important to emphasize how important it is to clarify all the issues already at the offer preparation and negotiation stage. At this point, the project team, together with the project manager, potentially have the greatest chance of 'setting' the project for the future. For this reason, a project manager must be selected and appointed during the sales process, and a potential project team must be organized at the same time. The relevant departments responsible for the subsequent implementation of the work also need to be involved.

A project manager and project team involved in the offer preparation process and contract negotiations perceive the project differently. They can read the client's intentions very clearly. They know the origins of the various provisions in the contract, whether they concern the scope, the timeline, or project objectives. They understand the risks and can come up with appropriate strategies and solutions. They have a chance to meet the key people on the client side. Even before the work starts, they learn about the client's organization and build important relationships that can be useful later.

Alternatively, when the project manager and the team are only appointed after the contract has been signed, all the mentioned events or processes do not happen. People have to learn about the project from scratch. The contract has to be explained to them. It is a process that resembles a game of Chinese whispers. Someone participated in the sales process, listened to the customer, negotiated, wrote something down, and finally, someone else passed it on to the people delivering the project.

There is a huge difference between a team that has a good understanding of the client, their organization, objectives, and the contract itself before the project starts and a team that does not have this knowledge and has to learn everything about the client from scratch or that has to look for some essential information in the contract. After all, it is very often the case that you encounter a problem during the project, and then you need to track down the person who signed the contract or submitted the offer to discuss with them what it was all about in the first place.

Involving the project team in drafting the proposal, sales discussions, and negotiations protects the company from many risks. Business analysts can describe the scope well, set the right objectives, limit the client's demands and expectations, and ensure the future stream of additional assignments (i.e., CRs). Engineers, architects, and implementation consultants can accurately define the scope of integration with external systems, migration, and testing. It's common knowledge to know how these areas like to slip through the cracks and how often clients fail to describe these processes, overlook them, or are simply unaware of the problems and complexity of the implementation on their side.

What's more, it is at the time of signing the contract that the client's organization is most flexible. Then, once the project has started, it becomes more rigid. Later, it becomes impossible to include new provisions, clarify open issues, make the responsibilities more detailed, protect the vendor against scope creep, and so forth. **Thus, the only time to make satisfactory arrangements is during sales and contract negotiations.**

Since we have the most influence on all the parameters of the project during the offer preparation process and negotiations, we need to use this time well. If we leave negotiations solely in the hands of the sales or legal team, what will they focus on? What are they going to pay attention to? I don't mean to blame or criticize anyone.

But, the general truth is that our professional experience, the bonus system in which we operate, and the objectives imposed on us all greatly impact what we focus on when negotiating a contract with a client. Therefore, the sales and legal team will focus largely on completing the negotiations as quickly as possible and on the financial and legal parameters, often in great detachment from the project or implementation aspects.

If you want to be sure that the project will have good parameters, that someone will ensure that the timeline is realistic, that the scope of the project is written down accurately and carefully, that the quality and acceptance criteria are realistic, that the SLA parameters are realistic, and so forth, then you need to make sure that specialists in this area are assigned to these tasks, and by specialists I mean the actual project team! This team must also be interdisciplinary from the outset, with holistic expertise in the future project's key parameters.

For example, during the negotiation of a very large IT project, which would cost tens of thousands of man-days, an interdisciplinary team was set up from the start. It comprised leaders who would later be responsible for delivering the various elements of the scope. The process of drafting the proposal, negotiating, and preparing the preliminary analysis took almost a year. The result was a contract that was more than a thousand pages long!

Even though the project was extremely complex, despite delays, pivots, changes in scope, project management strategy, subcontractor swaps, and changes in the client's organization, it was successful from the client's point of view and, most importantly, in this context, very profitable from the vendor's point of view, which kept the best people on the project throughout. All this was possible thanks to the work the project team did at the offer preparation and negotiation stage, even before the contract was signed and the project formally started!

Involving the project team in the offer preparation and negotiation process also increases transparency and the quality of the decisions made by the company.

By adding people to the sales process—specialists in all aspects of delivering and then maintaining the developed IT system, you make sure that, as a company, you have a complete and real picture of the situation (or at least something close to it). Therefore, you can make a conscious decision whether you agree to the client's terms or renegotiate them. For example, if the specialists object to the delivery schedule, you will either have to extend it and renegotiate with the client or deliberately accept it but already understand and accept the risks involved.

If, on the other hand, the team demonstrates that the project will be largely unprofitable and at the same time suggests an amount by which to increase the valuation (pricing) of the work, the company will also then be able to decide whether to accept the losses in the future or to decide to make one more attempt to renegotiate the financial terms at the risk of not signing the contract with the new client.

There are, of course, contracts signed at short notice just to meet the sales targets. For example, while negotiating a contract for a large company in Europe, the comments and suggestions of the development and implementation departments were completely ignored. Six months after the start of work, the project entered escalation mode, and practically all of the management responsible for its implementation resigned from the company. The timeline was unrealistic. The promised functionality could not be developed in the time planned. The project was in a state of escalation for the next one and a half years and barely survived two attempts by the client to terminate the contract. It was eventually delivered, but the third implementation team did this after a two-year delay and at a significant financial loss.

Finally, there's a very important point that must not be forgotten. Despite the enthusiasm of winning a new client, you must ensure that you have the option to discontinue the project and exit the contract.

We can never be sure exactly how cooperation with a given client will turn out, what kind of people we will encounter, how mature and professional the client will be, whether their expectations correspond to the real needs of the organization, how this will translate into the scope of work, schedule, and costs.

Therefore, during the negotiations, it is imperative to ensure that you can finish the cooperation in the future if this is the only sensible path from a business point of view! Contracts without such a safety mechanism should not be signed at all!

We can take as an example two large projects in which the vendors failed to ensure that the contract could be terminated in a crisis. In both cases, vendors signed contracts, allowing their clients to interpret the scope subjectively. The actual costs tripled! The vendors suffered huge financial losses and, at the same time, for a long time, they had no legal possibility to effectively exit the costly and unprofitable projects. In one example, thanks to the unprofitable contract, the vendor eventually acquired new, this time already profitable projects in other companies in the same capital group.

In the second example, however, the project did not make the slightest sense financially, neither from a product development nor new customer acquisition point of view, as this was the only implementation of the IT system.

In the euphoria of acquiring a new customer, our thinking is rarely cool enough to consider that we may one day want to terminate the contract and stop the project. Unfortunately, such thinking can potentially lead to disaster!

Therefore, if the project to be carried out is expected to be very difficult, large, complex, run in a hostile environment, with significant revenues, involving significant financial resources and a large team, it is imperative that you get involved in the offer preparation and negotiation process. This applies to the project manager, the future project team, and all the departments potentially involved in delivering the project!

The first rule of running impossible projects is to "get involved in the contract negotiations." This is the most you can do to influence the kind of project and environment you will work in and the chances of success!

CHAPTER 9

Rule 2: Define What It Means to "Deliver" the Project

It is not necessary to change. Survival is not mandatory.

—William Edwards Deming

Every project manager is taught from the beginning of their career that a well-run project is one in which the entire scope of work is delivered on time and with expected quality. This is the most commonly repeated mantra: scope, time, quality. These, of course, are set out in the sacred contract, which is, after all, the primary and only interpretation of how things should be done. And so much for the theory.

In practice, the success of a project is not only about delivering everything according to the contract.

The contract defines how the client envisioned the goals and success of the project at the time it was signed. However, that wouldn't be accurate, either. The contract usually describes the client's expectations, which the client defined when deciding to start the purchasing process. From this point onward, the client's expectations and the project's success criteria begin to evolve. In the case of large and complex projects, it usually takes

© Marcin Dąbrowski 2025
M. Dąbrowski, *10 Rules for Impossible Projects*,
https://doi.org/10.1007/979-8-8688-1463-1_9

from one and a half to two years from the preparation and approval of the business plan for the launch of the project, through the initiation and execution of the tender process to the signing of the contract with the selected vendor! The passage of time during this period brings about a lot of changes. The business environment changes, the organization develops, and the clients' needs do, too—not to mention the learning process and evolution of the client's organization. When the need to launch a project arises, there is a vision that the client builds on certain assumptions.

Then, over time, it turns out that the vision is evolving, that some assumptions were wrong, that others need to be changed, and that others still need to be added. What the vendor perceives during the course of the work as a demanding attitude on the part of the client, who keeps adding new requirements, usually has nothing to do with a bad attitude on the part of the client but rather with a learning process on his part.

The client had simply not been aware of the complexity of certain issues and is now only gradually, step by step, discovering what their expectations should be. If, in such a case, you stick to the execution of the contract to the dot, this can lead to disaster.

Let's take a closer look at a couple of project examples. In the first one, the project was carried out exactly as agreed upon. However, the client did not want to pay for the project. It turned out that they completely misunderstood how the implemented solution should be used. They did not know how to configure it and, therefore, did not see the added value. On the other hand, the vendor insisted on invoicing for the work they had contractually completed. The situation was a stalemate and almost verged on taking legal action.

Eventually, a new, more conciliatory project manager was appointed, and some time was spent proactively helping the client to tailor the platform to their needs. As a result, the client approved the delivery of the work and paid for it. As can be seen in this case, sticking to the theoretical principles of project management, that is, getting the work done on time, in scope, and with the right quality, almost led to disaster.

In the second example, the situation was more complicated. A contract was signed, and it became increasingly unprofitable as time passed. The project was taking more time than expected. The vendor was reducing the size of their team because of the losses he was incurring.

The client also seriously underestimated the work that needed to be done on his side. After two years, one of the three planned phases of the project was delivered. The project was then stopped, and the commissioned part of the system was deployed. Interestingly, it turned out that the implementation of barely 30% of the planned scope was enough to meet virtually all of the client's expectations. In this case, it is also clear how strongly the initial project goals can evolve and how they can deviate from the ones described in the contract.

Finally, in the third example, a contract was signed to implement a new IT platform in an international constellation of several subsidiaries of a larger group. After two years of the project, it became apparent that the client's main problem was not the IT platform itself but rather a problem with data extraction from several different systems over which the client had no control. So, an additional project was launched with a third-party company, which ultimately failed to deal with the data extraction issue, consequently stopping both projects.

A feasible move on the part of the vendor could have been to take full responsibility for data preparation. However, this was not done, and the project failed. The vendor seemingly stuck correctly to their role and the objectives defined in the contract. As can be seen, this did not help at all. The problem was that the project's success criteria changed dramatically during the project, and the vendor did not want to accept this, as they saw themselves as an IT system manufacturer and did not want to enter the IT services (data extraction) area.

Based on these three examples, you can see that the client's goals and expectations defined in the contract versus the actual ones are often completely different. The longer the project lasts, the more divergent they can become (even though, in theory, they should be the same).

Moreover, "delivering the project" is often understood differently by the client and the vendor; for example, for the client, it may mean deploying one or more milestones within a certain timeframe, the successful replacement of an old system with a new one, the achievement of certain KPIs, an increase in organizational efficiency, the possibility of reducing staff, and so forth. However, the vendor may, for example, be aiming at a long-running project in which the client keeps paying extra by commissioning new requirements. For the vendor, a good project is also one where basic functionality is delivered at the end of the project. Then, the client pays for the development of additional features over several years.

For example, very often, after a certain period of time has elapsed since the work started, for various reasons, it turns out that the project is not feasible within the budget or timeframe. The client usually doesn't pay attention to this. They push to continue the work according to the contractual timeline without a significant increase in budget. From the client's point of view, there have been no significant changes from the signed contract. From your company's perspective, however, the success criteria have changed dramatically. If the development of a system, platform, or product objectively has to take more time, the vendor will do everything to extend the project to buy more time. If, on top of that, a significant drop in profitability is an issue, they will probably stiffen their approach to analysis and be very uncompromising in their interpretation of the scope of work to generate as many CRs as possible.

From the point of view of the company responsible for carrying out the project, it is very often more beneficial to carry it out over a longer period of time but with a proportionately smaller team. This provides greater stability in resource planning.

Finally, if the vendor is suffering continuous losses and is unable to communicate with the client, their definition of success may be to suspend or stop the project.

In contrast, the client still expects to deliver the system or parts of it according to the schedule defined in the contract. So, it is not at all the case that delivering the scope of the project on time and to the right quality is the success criterion for both parties. The criteria for success or the definition of delivering the project evolve on both the client and vendor side. These are very often completely different, divergent directions of change.

In other words, the longer a project lasts, the more the definition of project delivery potentially deviates from what was set out in the contract. Therefore, not only does it change on each side, but the interests of the client and the vendor can become completely different to the extent that one side seeks to implement the system as quickly as possible. In contrast, the other seeks to get out of the contract as quickly as possible.

The following are examples of changes introduced by the client and how they affect the definition of the successful delivery of the project.

- **The client may move away from a Big Bang strategy (implementing the entire scope at one point), breaking the project into several stages, with each milestone having a specific business value.**

  In such a case, it most often turns out that delivering a specific milestone (rather than the entire project as per the contract) is crucial for the client, allowing them to declare success within their organization and, at the same time, is the point of no return, where, regardless of subsequent events, the client is no longer able to withdraw from such a project.

  The project manager must have a thorough understanding of the preceding changes. This way, they can focus the team's efforts on a specific goal, achieve it, and secure the project. The focus should then be on delivering a selected element of the scope, a specific stage of greatest value to the client. This is, by the way, a very good strategy in large and complex, unrealistic projects, in which we learn from the beginning the absurdity of the schedule in the contract.

It is then necessary to determine very quickly what the client's biggest problem is, what could solve most of their problems, and then try to adapt the scope and timeline of individual milestones accordingly,

- **The client may let go of certain goals that are unrealistic from the vendor's point of view.** For example, they may aim to replace only a part of the current architecture of the systems (and not all of it). They may migrate only a subset of customers to the new system and not all of them at once. In that case, the criteria for delivering the project changed dramatically.

We can significantly increase the chances of success if we are very careful and regularly analyze what the project's success means to the client. In one project, the client initially planned to launch an IT platform that would enable the planning of mobile networks in all technologies (2G, 3G, and 4G) and simultaneously for all equipment suppliers (Nokia, Ericsson, ZTE, etc.).

Mildly put, the undertaking did not seem quite unrealistic, but it was really ridiculous. Expecting dozens of IT systems to be replaced in one and a half years was wishful thinking. However, it turned out that most problems were solved by replacing a specific group of systems with 4G technology, which was the pillar of the strategy for the coming years. The hardware for it was only supplied by one company.

Appropriate new objectives were set, the scope was narrowed down and focused on the most important aspects for the client, and the project was a great success.

Of course, it was a completely different project from the one that had been started! The scope, schedule, priorities, project phases, business environment, and other aspects changed. The key to success was ongoing communication with the client about their business goals and the right adaptation of the delivery strategy.

- **The client may run out of money and want to suspend the project, extend it, limit it, or reduce the scope.** Although this happens often, it is rarely communicated to vendors. The vendor's strategy for delivering the project will be completely different if the client temporarily reduces the project budget, different if the client wants to extend the project, and still different if you expect the work to be stopped and the contract terminated.

All these aspects are strongly linked to the client's business situation. If the client is forced to change their business strategy, it will directly impact our project. And so, in one project, a large company was preparing for a sale, which meant that the time to make changes to the IT systems environment shrank accordingly. Overnight, the client turned the delivery schedule of individual milestones upside down.

Yet, the vendor still wanted to deliver the project in accordance with the contract provisions. Within weeks, the project was permanently suspended. Therefore, you need to understand at all times what the success of the project means for your client, what it means for your company, and whether and how these visions are aligned,

- **Along the way, the client may lose the business case for continuing the work.** If this is the case, the vendor needs to manage the project very skillfully so as not to generate friction and escalation or requests for budget increases, which can only make the client think twice about whether the whole project makes sense.

Counterintuitively, most large transformation projects planned over several years become pointless after the first two years. However, clients carry them on for the next few years until either the budget runs out (and decisions have to be made to stop) or a decision-maker who has the courage to question the sense of continuing the work is found.

One of the most interesting situations was when a project was stopped during the production switchover procedure! After two years of work, during the data migration, the client realized that there was no point in running the new system! The project manager must always monitor what it means for the client to deliver the project. In this case, this was neglected.

Of course, if the client does not see the point in continuing the work, you have a non-trivial issue to resolve. Although developing a strategy at that point is difficult, you should be prepared to react to the situation.

It is not often talked about, but it's equally important to monitor the business sense of the project, its goal, and the success criteria from the vendor's point of view! Although it might not seem like that, the vendor's interests may not be aligned with the client's expectations.

Both parties are usually well synchronized on the day of signing the contract. With time, however, the vendor's and the client's perspectives often become misaligned. The root cause of this situation is the mistakes made by both parties during the bidding and negotiation process when the project is shaped, estimated, and described. Some problems and challenges arise objectively or are not foreseen. Added to all this is the volatility of the business environment.

That's why it's important to realize that the definition of successful completion of the project may also evolve on the vendor's side. The following are some examples.

- **The vendor may, for a variety of reasons (mainly financial), want to leave the project or "choke" it, which means limiting their involvement to the minimum necessary.** If the project has been underestimated or the client requires much more than expected (and the scope is described in very general terms), it may turn out that paying penalties and going to court pays off more than continuing with a loss-making project.

   Then, success and "delivering" the project may be a skillful exit from the contract, going to court and stopping the work or suspending the project.

- **Success can mean skillfully negotiating and winning extra money for the project.** If a project is unprofitable, it is the management's job to improve the financial situation, not whether the client is satisfied.

It sounds brutal, but it is the sad truth. The people involved in the project must be paid their salaries! Therefore, the aim is to improve the economic situation of the project, and nobody pays attention to what is to be delivered and when!

Clients often do not realize how big and how much of a negative impact the project's financial situation has. They expect the vendor to do everything to deliver on time while they are dealing with completely different problems! Ultimately, the client incurs much higher costs because the project is delayed than if they had agreed with the vendor. After all, if the project takes longer, you have to pay for the cost of the systems that were not switched off. You have to pay the cost of your own team and the like.

Unfortunately, there is still an attitude in the market in which clients waste more money and time trying to ruthlessly stick to the terms of the contract than they would if they were flexible about the vendors' financial problems, which, after all, are mainly due to the way the bidding and negotiation process is conducted and not to bad will.

- **Success can mean continuing the work endlessly to keep being needed and ensure the continuous flow of cash, rather than finishing the project and simply disappearing.** Very often, from the vendor's point of view, implementing the product or system itself is hardly profitable. Only after the deployment to production does the most profitable period come. This is when the client commissions extensions and new system functionalities over many years.

The process of valuing new functionalities is itself very deterministic and accurate. You then have to deal with a large number of carefully estimated changes. You understand the client's expectations, problems, and working environment better. Therefore, all this work is profitable, unlike the earlier system implementation period, when both parties put some assumptions in the contract based on very limited data.

It is for this reason that, even though during the course of the project, clients would like to take care of all their business needs in the project price, vendors try to deliver only the necessary minimum per the contract terms so that they can later make money from extensions to the implemented system. This should not be surprising.

However, it must be understood that, at this point, the criteria for delivering the project are different for both the client and the vendor. One side wants to get as much as possible in the shortest possible time for the lowest possible price, while the other side has a completely different vision.

- **Success may also be creating a new product or entering a new market**. In such cases, the vendor may care more about building a relationship, client satisfaction, and preparing the ground for getting recommendations as a partner to other companies in the region.

Sticking to the scope, schedule, or cost (within reason) tends to become less important. For example, if you want to build a new product, you cannot be rigorous or uncompromising in controlling the scope. After all, you are interested in gaining information on the future practical application of the product developed from scratch.

Interestingly, clients often willingly opt for such projects. On the one hand, they have to wait longer for the results. On the other hand, they have a very strong influence on the development of the product and ultimately receive a system perfectly tailored to their business needs.

The point is that completing the project according to the contract terms is not a guarantee of success. The attempts to stick to the contract by the dot may even obscure the image of reality, making you blind to the key changes in both the client's and your own organization's expectations (if you work for the vendor).

Success criteria and completion of the project have to be closely monitored, analyzed and changed on an ongoing basis. Then, depending on those criteria, you need to adapt and adjust the management approach, priorities, style of communication, and so forth.

An extreme example of the variability of client expectations involved a project where the same IT platform from the same vendor was implemented four times over ten years. The first three attempts failed, primarily because the business users did not utilize the system after its implementation. In each instance, the vendor delivered everything according to the contract, yet it did not help. Only on the fourth attempt did both parties precisely define what was truly critical from the client's perspective, what constitutes project success, and what the vendor's criteria for successful delivery were. Ultimately, the client received what they genuinely needed rather than contractually wanted.

The success criteria and project delivery must be constantly analyzed and modified. The definition of these terms in a given project continuously evolves on both the client's and the vendor's side.

The following questions should be continuously asked: What does the client care about? What is most important to them? What will make the project be considered a success? Does the client still want to continue with the work? Does the project still hold value for them? Similarly, you need to think in the context of your own organization: What does our company care about? Why is this project being continued? On what basis do we assess its success? Should we continue this project, and if not, why not?

It's worth pointing out that none of these questions are directly related to the contract terms or the classic project triangle: scope, time, and quality. These are more fundamental questions. Depending on the answers you get, you will shape the scope and schedule of work further, as well as the relationship with the client, the way of communication, and the level of cost involvement. In other words, everything should be adjusted to the current definition of project success, both from the client's perspective and yours.

In summary, throughout the life of a project, you need to be mindful of what success means for both parties at any given time. You should always consider changing objectives and how to keep an eye on them to avoid a situation where the contract is delivered as written. The client is still unsatisfied, does not pay, or terminates the contract prematurely.

There should be an ongoing business dialogue with as many significant people as possible at multiple levels of both organizations.

To understand the client's changing business objectives, you first need to know about them and their priorities, and so you need to talk to the client, "absorb" their environment, attend their internal meetings, go to lunches and dinners, establish informal relationships—get as much information as possible from various, especially unofficial, sources.

Throughout this time, you should present a pro-client attitude and try to solve the client's problems rather than focusing on ruthlessly enforcing the contract. Only in such an environment is the client's team willing to trust you and openly communicate relevant issues.

You need to show commitment and a pragmatic attitude so that the client wants to work with you and is open to changing the contractual terms (including financial terms) to fit their new business priorities. The client must like you and see you as an added value. Then, they will demonstrate the right attitude, explain the goals, voice their expectations openly, and treat you as a trusted partner. Finally, they may also be willing to adjust the terms of the contract.

CHAPTER 10

Rule 3: Be Helpful and Show Commitment

If you love what you're doing and you always put the customer first, success will be yours.

—Raymond Kroc

You can read that most projects are delayed in various texts or study materials. Delivering projects by the book and perfectly is difficult, even when they seem simple or somewhat complicated. And what if the project you're dealing with is big and complex, and it's clear from the start that fulfilling the client's needs according to the contract is mildly ambitious or just plain unrealistic? And so, we're taught that the work should be completed on schedule at all costs, and the scope should be delivered in accordance with the provisions of the contract.

This is why everyone is focused primarily on the contract rather than the customer! They keep forgetting that the most important things for the customer are the style of cooperation with them, displaying the right attitude, and being proactive, engaged, and helpful!

© Marcin Dąbrowski 2025
M. Dąbrowski, *10 Rules for Impossible Projects*,
https://doi.org/10.1007/979-8-8688-1463-1_10

The outcome of the work is not the only criterion applied in vendor evaluation. In complex projects lasting several years, the deliverables are treated as being less important. From the client's point of view, a cooperative attitude is what counts most.

There are numerous instances of projects where the delivery of work based on the contract requirements not only displeased the client but also led to conflict. In one project, a system was delivered in accordance with the contract, but the client did not deploy the product to production because, as the work progressed, it became clear that his expectations were for something more complex. As long as the vendor insisted on meeting the requirements in the contract, the client refused to pay for the deliveries. Only when the vendor's attitude changed to one of openness and proactivity, of understanding the client's problem and trying to solve it, did the project begin to succeed. The client's expectations were out of scope, but if they had not been addressed, the matter would have ended up in court.

Another time in the project, which was supposed to last four years, it soon turned out that the client's business environment was changing like a kaleidoscope. The technology that was supposed to be supported by the implemented platform quickly became outdated. Some subcontractors left the market in this country, so some new ones were selected, but their way of working was completely different. All this called for adapting the newly designed system. In this case, the project was successful. It lasted much longer than expected, and if you were to compare the scope delivered to the scope described in the contract, you could conclude that a different project was delivered in relation to what was decided in the beginning!

Nevertheless, the client considered the entire undertaking a success. It was important to the client that the vendor's team was a partner, that they made an effort, were open to change, and solved problems.

The bigger the project, the more complex it is, and the longer it lasts, the less important it is whether you stick to the contract, and the more important it is what attitude you present and whether you are useful from the client's point of view!

Projects are run by people, people who can make mistakes. On the client side, in particular, these mistakes can be quite numerous. The larger the scope of the project, the greater the uncertainty, the longer the time horizon, the more dependencies there are, the higher the probability that someone will overlook an important detail, fail to take something into account, make a wrong assumption, and so forth. Later in the project, it is very easy to point out mistakes. But the project has to be completed.

That's why your attitude is key! You must be committed, proactive, and helpful. As a person, as a project manager, as a team member, and as a vendor. If someone likes you, respects you, trusts you, and wants to work with you (as they see value in it), they will always find a way to support you and try to help you put the project back on track.

If the problems cannot be objectively solved, the client can help you explain why you are behind schedule to their organization! Delays are not such a big issue. But it's extremely important, even more important, how the client sees you! If the client wants to work with you, they will explain to themselves that you made an effort, why it's not completely your fault, why the project will eventually be delivered, and the vendor can certainly cope with it!

Thus, instead of scrutinizing the contract, the scope, and the timeline, you should primarily focus on shaping your attitude toward the client.

Let's start with the first element of building a proactive or customer-centric attitude: engagement. Take, for example, a very large transformational project, which, in practice, shows the power of the right attitude and its impact on how the client perceives you. The project was sold to deliver the entire system within one and a half years. To a large extent, the client pushed for such an ambitious schedule. The vendor, however, knew from the beginning that this work schedule was unrealistic. As a result, the project team reported delays of another six months every quarter. Ultimately, the project did not last one and a half years but seven years! Interestingly, it ended successfully, and the client was very satisfied.

How is this even possible? Theoretically, the project should have been halted in a short time. You must analyze how the client and vendor worked together. From the very beginning, a great emphasis was placed on creating a unified team consisting of people from both sides, the client and the vendor. They built a team that worked in a harmonious, even friendly atmosphere.

Despite the pressure on deliveries, the project's importance in both organizations, and the problems within the team, full transparency, a high level of trust, and quick communication were maintained. In such an environment, problems, their objective causes, and possible strategies for action were openly discussed.

In every steering committee meeting with the client's and vendor's management, the project team explained with one voice where the delays came from, what problems they encountered, and what they would do about it. The client's management saw their team defending the project and the vendor, fighting for it and explaining that everything possible had been done objectively.

It is easy to see why the project continued and ultimately succeeded. If, in the same situation, the vendor's team had changed their attitude to passive, started arguing with the client that their requirements were too high, that they deviated from what was agreed in the contract, that certain things could not be achieved, the project would have ground to a halt.

In fact, this situation is very common.

In times of crisis, the client's management first looks at their team's reaction. They examine whether the people see the point in continuing the work and whether they still want to work with the vendor.

They also assess the attitude of the vendor's team, particularly the degree of their commitment to the client's business strategy. If this commitment is not shown, then you are asking for trouble. Nobody wants to work with people who don't care or show commitment!

It's worth noting that the issue of engagement has two facets. On the one hand, you need to be engaged, motivated, and work with passion. On the other hand, this engagement must be shown outwardly. Of course, both matters are closely related. Sometimes, you may be exhausted, demotivated, bored with the project, with the constantly recurring problems, or even discussions with the client, and so on.

However, you must outwardly show how much you care at critical moments! The client must see that you are making an effort. They should not have to guess or infer it. It must be self-evident!

It's best to start with yourself. If a project manager works passionately, makes an effort, and cares about the project, if they develop the habit of tackling and solving problems every day and derive pleasure from it, they don't have to think about proving anything. Their attitude and approach are clearly visible to the entire team. It's also noticeable for the client. This engaged attitude quickly spreads among the other project members. In a short time, they adopt all the behavioral patterns. It works similarly with the client. Even if the client is initially hostile, after a few meetings with an engaged vendor's team, the client's employees start working similarly, copying your behavior and approach.

What's more, after years, rather than remembering the project outcome, the clients tend to remember the vendor's attitude and feelings during the cooperation with their team. Whether the project was a success or a failure, if you demonstrated engagement and proactivity, were helpful, and did your best, the client will want to work with you again in the future—with you as a vendor and even more with you as an individual!

Similarly, this applies to your project team. If, as a project manager, you show engagement and a proactive attitude, if you take up the struggle every day, each person on your team can see it. People respect such an approach to work and life. They like to work with people who approach difficult situations positively. They also subconsciously take on the engagement, especially copying your attitude toward the client. If the project manager complains, speaks negatively about the client,

111

or does not trust them, then the whole team adopts a negative attitude and spreads defeatism in a short time. Such a project has little chance of success. However, if the project manager makes an effort and is motivated, then after some time, the team also adopts a positive attitude and fights every day.

Thus, engagement must be demonstrated on every level. You must show it as a business (vendor), as the management team, as the project leader, and as a person. It's important for every single individual to show engagement! It translates both into the potential success of the project and the current and future relationship with the client and each individual on their side.

Another element of the pro-client and proactive approach is being helpful. The client must perceive the cooperation with you as added value, both in terms of the delivered scope—a system or a product—and understanding the client's organization and problems.

It's extremely important whether the vendor goes beyond the defined terms and comes up with solutions. It's quite a common situation that a lot of the client's problems refer to areas outside the scope of the project. If, as a vendor, you try to suggest solutions even though it's not your obligation, you gain respect and create a very positive image in the client's eyes. Not only do you do your job, but you also give added value.

In such cases, clients start to see you as part of their team. When they have challenges (regardless of the project scope), they resort to you for advice. They value the conversations because they know that you will try to help them and suggest a solution.

As a result, your position as an individual and as a vendor becomes stronger. The project issues become less important. The client can't see a different option than continuing the cooperation—regardless of the challenges, delays, difficulties, or changes in the business environment. It's easy to see that the natural consequence of being helpful and proactive is increasing the volume of business with this particular client. Who will the client want to solve all their problems with? They are already discussing them with you anyway. It was you who suggested specific solutions. All this sounds great and seems simple when, in fact, it's very difficult and non-trivial.

There will always be two extremes and two poles in a project.

The client will insist on delivering according to the schedule and blame the vendor for delays; even those resulting from their actions will escalate problems to management. The natural reaction in such conditions is to try to defend yourself, thus shifting the blame onto the client, blaming them for the delays. It is extremely difficult to keep a cool head and stay calm, understand that the client is stressed, afraid of their managers' reactions, that it's nothing personal, that they have their own problems, and that instead of defending yourself, you should actually help them in this situation!

On the one hand, the client puts pressure on you, while on the other hand, they expect you to be helpful, useful, and engaged. Despite this, the client must feel that solving their problems is your priority.

In particular, you should not point out their mistakes, especially in meetings with the management. Of course, it is difficult to refrain from this in a working environment where the client is constantly building up pressure, and you feel attacked or cornered.

However, you need to remember that the client finances the project, and no one pays a vendor to prove to them their clumsiness or incompetence!

This type of behavior pattern soon leads to customer frustration. The vendor supposedly delivers everything according to the contract but hides its shortcomings under the pretext of delays or problems on the client's part (which often do occur), even worse, by blaming specific people on the client's side. This only leads to irritation or even hostility for those you work with. Instead of partners, you create enemies. It is only a matter of time before our behavior will reap a tragic harvest. It is important to remember that sooner or later, crisis situations will arise in a project when the client will have to make strategic decisions.

However, the client's management is always guided by the recommendations and opinions of their employees and their team. At such moments, it is crucial to know what individuals think of the vendor and specific team members, whether they perceive the vendor's attitude as useful, and whether it brings value.

That's why you need to aim at making the client dependent on you! You need to take ownership of their tasks, especially the ones that are not easy for the client, and take over their competencies so that it becomes impossible to solve problems without you.

It is at this moment that your company becomes somewhat safe. The more pressure you take off the client's shoulders, the more ownership you take, the more linked you are to their organization, and the longer the relationship with the client will last!

You should not be afraid to take ownership of the client's problems! It does not put you in any kind of danger but rather stabilizes or strengthens your position in their eyes.

Unfortunately, such an approach still isn't commonly understood. The basis of this situation lies in sticking to the classical principles of the project management theory. So, the project must be delivered on time. It doesn't matter that, for example, the client has difficulties on their side. That's even better! You can hide your own problems using the delays on the client's side as an excuse! Regrettably, this is a classic in project management.

A typical example is a project where the vendor implements or develops an IT system while the client prepares and migrates the data. Virtually always, the client has problems with data migration, with the lack of data, its poor quality, interpretation, lack of competencies, or people on their side who even have any idea about what kind of data can be found in which systems, if and for what it is needed, and how to interpret it. In a project like this, the client would be very happy to eliminate the responsibility for migrating data. They'd leave it to the vendor and pay for the extra work.

The standard thinking on the vendor's side is like this: according to the contract, we're responsible for implementing the product. Why would you take on additional, risky tasks? The client is facing problems, the project is delayed, and it's the client's fault, so you have more time to catch up on work. Unfortunately, this kind of attitude is recommended by project management theories!

The signed contract clearly states what is supposed to be delivered and when. The problem is that the client doesn't care about what was written in the contract. They have problems to deal with; they hadn't anticipated them, and they expect a partnership rather than exposing their incompetence or—even worse—a situation when the vendor takes advantage of the client's problems. If you understand that your attitude is more important for the client, alongside your proactive approach, engagement, and meeting the client's needs, your point of view completely changes. It suddenly becomes clear that it's worth taking responsibility for some extra tasks.

Let's take the data migration as an example. Is it really the case that if the vendor takes responsibility for data migration, their situation worsens because all potential problems are on their side? Of course not! The vendor's position actually strengthens. The client is fully reliant on the vendor in this project! Even if the vendor faces difficulties with the data migration, it won't matter!

First, the client will understand that they would face the same objective issues themselves. Second, they will be pleased that they don't have to deal with this tedious task. Third, the client will be even more dependent on the vendor! The hypothetical replacement of the vendor with a new one will be even more challenging. After all, a new company must be found to take over the data migration.

It turns out that it doesn't make any sense. The current vendor has already done a tremendous amount of work to analyze the client's existing systems, the data structure of each, the data connections between those systems, technology, and so forth. Suddenly, it becomes clear that taking on additional responsibilities (of course, for additional compensation), tasks outside the contractual scope, makes sense and perfectly secures the vendor's interests (and does not threaten them).

That is why you have to solve as many problems as possible on the client side. You have to make them dependent on your competence and your team!

You need to take responsibility for the technological challenges and product challenges and take on additional roles or parts of the business process so that you become an integral part of the client organization!

The more dependent the client is on you, the more difficult it becomes to operate without you. All this is contrary to thinking in terms of "in or out of scope of the project."

So, if you are helpful, the client always sees the value in working with you. If you are committed and the client sees that you care and are doing everything you can to help them achieve their goals, it is not necessarily related to this project. Finally, if you are so valuable that the client is dependent on you, they will want to continue working with you at all costs, regardless of whether the project is progressing according to the terms of the contract, whether it is behind schedule or encountering difficulties!

Therefore, always be helpful and constantly show your commitment!

CHAPTER 11

Rule 4: Build Relationships and the Power of Influence

You can have everything in life you want if you will just help enough other people get what they want.

—Zig Ziglar

Rule number four goes: build relationships and the power of influence. At first glance, it may seem completely unrelated to project management. In practice, however, whether you apply it or not will impact the project's success or failure.

Let's look at what project members usually focus on, which they intuitively perceive as completing tasks. It begins with an analysis of what should be done and when. Data repositories are created, and then there are systems for task management and monitoring progress. Most people carry out technical tasks. They design and develop systems or products that are later tested. Indeed, there are also project meetings, but their main focus is on discussing progress and deliverables, and the discussion is based on the contents of the project management systems, documents, spreadsheets, and reports. And this is all good.

© Marcin Dąbrowski 2025
M. Dąbrowski, *10 Rules for Impossible Projects*,
https://doi.org/10.1007/979-8-8688-1463-1_11

The problem is that it's not enough. Everything seems to be under control. You seem to be monitoring how the deliverables reflect the requirements in the project documentation or task management systems. And then you go to a meeting with the client, complacent and supposedly prepared (everything matches what was put in the contract after all), yet the client says that everything has changed and they are not interested in any of that data! Some people might think it's ridiculous. Unfortunately, that's what it's like.

The project is not documentation. The project is not a task management system. The project is not a spreadsheet or report. The project is a constellation of people from two interrelated businesses. The worst thing is that instead of focusing on those people, we tend to confine ourselves to the comfort of closed rooms and work with the documentation and the internal task management systems.

Instead of listening to your peers on the client side, rather than building relationships with them, try to understand them as people, their ambitions, needs, see what's important for them, what they will achieve in a given project, what their preferences are in terms of work, what they're good at and where they feel uncertain, you choose to escape to the cozy habit of working in separation from the customer.

For example, a project for one of the largest companies in Great Britain was carried out perfectly, according to the terms of the contract, without any significant escalations. After almost two years, during one of the steering committee meetings, the client said that although they were impressed by the vendor's performance, they needed to change the sequence of the project phases completely. Effectively, the entire project needed to be started from scratch!

Of course, the vendor's team and the client's team communicated on a regular basis. There were project meetings. They were monitoring progress. They were discussing risks and challenges. The problem was that nobody built a personal relationship with the client's management team. The discussions were only about the formal side of the project. Their main focus was on the timeline and the technical aspects.

Unfortunately, such discussions don't provide you with any other type of information. If some effort had been put into building informal or even friendly relationships, most of the key people on the client side would have shared their doubts about the project. They would have spilled the tea about their talks with the business and the management team. The vendor would have found out earlier that the client was not sure about their delivery strategy and that a completely different approach was being considered, so if those relationships had been built early enough, a lot of time and money would have been saved, which would have otherwise been wasted.

In another project in Germany, the client, at a certain point, declared during the steering committee meeting that they decided to reduce the scope of the project and the scope of maintenance services provided by the vendor. This decision would result in a significant revenue drop for the vendor. Such a decision was against the terms of the contract, so the vendor initially considered a confrontational scenario. However, in this case, the crisis was resolved mainly due to informal relationships. After several one-on-one meetings, a mutually beneficial solution was worked out. The vendor agreed to the client's proposal, and in return, a few months later, they were hired to provide services in another area.

Finally, the third example illustrates the power of building relationships and influence. In a large project involving several subcontractors of the client, escalations and delays were occurring constantly. The client was implementing a new system designed to introduce precise control over business processes and allow the client to accurately account for the subcontractors' work.

Naturally, these companies were working to disrupt, delay, and block the project. The problem was that the vendor of the new IT system was a new element of this constellation, while the subcontractors had been working with the client for over 15 years. Each time the new platform vendor was delayed with their scope of work, the other companies cleverly exploited this fact. Fortunately, the vendor team and management had built close and friendly relationships with their client counterparts. It was only through informal communication channels and a large amount of mutual trust that this project was ultimately brought to completion.

Thus, building and maintaining relationships with the client is very important. From the beginning, you should establish informal communication channels with individual people on the client's side. Moreover, this matter does not only concern the project manager. You must establish such communication channels at every managerial and operational level. In a sense, every person interacting with the client should be responsible for "making friends" with the individuals they work with.

Analysts, architects, programmers, quality engineers, project managers, directors, or the board—each of these people should form informal relationships with their counterparts on the client's side! This approach will pay off in the future.

It significantly speeds up the work pace, improves the cooperation climate, streamlines communication, enhances understanding, prevents unnecessary misunderstandings, and prevents escalations. In crisis situations, it is a very effective lifeline.

It often happens that we can turn our partners on the client's side into good colleagues or even friends. **However, you must always remember that you are in a client-vendor relationship. Therefore, you have obligations that you must fulfill. The client pays you, so you need to try harder, help more, and show greater patience and understanding.**

You should remember that situations will arise in which you will be pressured, attacked, and feel cheated, and a certain boundary of honesty or fair play will be crossed. Even then, you must keep your cool and remember that you work in the vendor role, and you're expected to be fully professional. Sometimes, you must listen to the client's tirades and accept their game even if, in your opinion, it is not fair. Remember that the informal relationships you have created are much more important than a momentary or even longer crisis. One thing is certain: your attitude and care for relationships with individual people always pay off. Always! There are no exceptions to this rule.

In most cases, the behavior of individual people on the client's side, which, from your (subjective) point of view, seems ungraceful, results from the constraints they face within their organization. In other words, they are often put in a no-win situation and must act in a particular way. Or you simply don't understand them. If you have built informal relationships, sooner or later, these people tell you over coffee or lunch why they acted in such a way. Sometimes, they even explain to you in confidence what may happen in the project so that you can prepare for it appropriately.

While building informal relationships, you should try to become a trusted adviser so the client is willing to share their issues with you. You need to make a significant effort to deserve this kind of respect and openness. You can't achieve that by your eloquence alone. You must prove in action that you are helpful and care about solving problems.

If you act like this, the client will be willing to share the information with you. You need to remember that for this to happen, you need to take care of the informal relationships. If you only solve problems but are not looking for opportunities to meet and talk informally, no relationships will be built, and they should be built intentionally. On no account can it be left to chance.

It is often forgotten that power struggles also occur on the client's side. Individuals have their own agendas, pursuing their own plans, which may not align with the project's objectives you are working on. The fact that the client signed a contract with you results from someone (an individual or a group of people) in their organization wanting to achieve specific results in the future. However, this state of affairs was true when the contract was signed. Immediately afterward, the balance of power can shift at any given moment.

Project management manuals usually do not mention this, nor do they explain that parallel to the project's implementation, processes in the client's organization can lead to its termination, regardless of the results.

It is enough, for example, for a key managing person to change and bring a different vision of development in the area that concerns you. For example, in one of the European companies, the IT team was carrying out a portfolio of projects according to a strategy outlined by a director who was planning to retire. The person who was to replace him was 20 years younger, ambitious, and had aspirations of joining the company's board in a short time. Their goal was to stand out, separate from the previous strategy, and implement their own new and, of course, "better" one. In such a configuration, the fate of most projects run by the client's IT organization was uncertain. It did not matter whether this or that project was bringing the expected outcomes or whether the vendors were meeting the contractual terms. The only defense for each of them was to quickly establish relations with the new management, which in a few months was to take the helm and decide on the new IT strategy.

You must remember that regardless of what stands in the contract or whether you are delivering substantively, fulfilling obligations, solving problems, and so on, you must build relationships at every level.

Even within the project, there may be certain kinds of power struggles. Some people will be favorable to you, while others could obstruct you. Some people may be very important; others may be very loud, but their opinions won't matter. Certain individuals will have a very significant impact on the PR and perception of your project. Therefore, you must establish a relationship with all these people, particularly those who seem to be your adversaries and try turning them into your allies.

It is also very important to establish relationships at the managerial level in the project's early days when there is mutual enthusiasm after signing the contract and the anticipation of an exciting challenge.

If you do not build relationships between the management teams (especially the boards) of both companies at the beginning of the project, it will be extremely difficult to establish these relationships in a crisis situation when things go wrong, and those relationships are needed.

At that point, the climate won't be right for getting to know each other. In crisis moments, when companies entrench themselves behind formal letters, adopting very firm and confrontational positions, nothing is more helpful than the possibility of having an informal meeting or phone conversation between the management or key decision-makers of both companies. The biggest project problems are often solved over coffee, lunch, or dinner when you can talk informally face-to-face and articulate your position and the motivations and constraints behind it without consequences.

A very good practice is involving the management teams of both companies in the project by arranging regular steering committee meetings with the right highly influential individuals. Of course, the best venue for such events is the client's (or the vendor's) headquarters, and then a follow-up in the form of dinner. In this way, you ensure that relationships on every level are built and involve the management of your own company in the project. It is often the case that the management team at your company gets annoyed by the problems in the project. They criticize your actions, put pressure on you, refuse to understand what the problem is, and, at the same time, do not provide the necessary resources.

So, they demand solutions but do not offer you the right means or the ability to act. If such a manager or board member is invited to the steering committee at the client's, where they have to explain the plan and take personal ownership of the promises they make, it soon turns out that they have changed their mind and show more understanding of the problems in the project or with the client and they become your ally. Not only do they stop criticizing and making it difficult, but they also start supporting you. Involving executives in steering committee meetings is one of the most effective strategies for ensuring internal support for your project.

Also, it shouldn't be forgotten that building relationships and influence within your own company is perhaps even more important than with the client's team.

There's also corporate politics at play in your own organization. Individuals and executives have their own agendas and goals. Each of them cares about something and tries to achieve something. They each have their own motives. For example, a given manager may care about the stability of the outcome and does not want to give away or transfer their people to our risky project. Others may be promotion-oriented and avoid any venture that they feel may jeopardize their unblemished upward path. Still, others will see a vested interest in your project or helping you as a person. So, beyond the project itself, you have to consider that there is a level of "politics" in your company, a game in which you participate whether you want it or not. So, if you have no choice, you must consciously navigate this environment, read the situation, and use it appropriately for the good of the project and the client. You may take offense and think you are above it, but such an approach will, unfortunately, do you no good. You should be pragmatic—instead of criticizing it, you should be able to use the system.

If you want to have access to the best people in the company, to the right financial resources, and to an additional budget, you need to build relationships with the decision-makers in the company. On the one hand, your goal should be individuals with the appropriate authority and the power to act. On the other hand, you should also talk to all the managers affected by your project, especially those who will support you with "their" people or resources. It is not enough to rely on a board member who will "order" a given manager to support your project with resources. After all, such a manager will, by definition, assign the weakest individuals, as their own goals will guide them.

Therefore, you also need to establish a relationship with this manager and try to show them that they can benefit from participating in your project. Management textbooks do not write about how much work it takes for a project manager to organize and then maintain a project team that is targeted throughout the project, as other managers constantly try to acquire people for their projects at the expense of your team.

To build and maintain a project team, you must nurture relationships with as many key people in your company as possible.

Similarly, the same applies to crisis situations, both in your project and in the entire company. For example, if the situation in the project escalates, the client escalates, putting pressure on your company's management. It may quickly turn out that your personal position, or the position of individual team members, is at risk. Management has the unpleasant tendency to blame specific individuals, regardless of the true causes of the problem. Therefore, if the situation in the project escalates and you have not built relationships with decision-makers in your company, unfortunately, you will fear for your fate in the organization.

However, if you have spent time nurturing personal relationships with key managers and keeping them informed in informal conversations about the project status and potential risks, you can usually feel safe, and the conversation about problems becomes more substantive. The same happens when your organization has limited resources and needs to prioritize one project over another.

On the one hand, it might seem that such decisions are made based on numbers and objective data; on the other hand, you need to remember that each point of view is subjective. The management team receives information and reports from specific managers, and each of them has their own agenda and goals. Thus, they present the data in a subjective, personally beneficial way.

In theory, each company has its financial reports. But you can't put a whole business into an Excel spreadsheet. There is always some context, opportunities, risks, relations, and ongoing discussions with the client. And that's why this space is usually occupied by people who promote their own agenda within the company. So, if you want to avoid a situation when your team members are being taken away from you and moved to another project, you need to nurture the relationships with the decision-makers so that their image of your project and its impact is right.

A better image of your project (in your own company) directly impacts.

- The importance of the project in the organization

- Availability of resources

- The management's willingness to spend money on the project and invest

- The project's priority during a potential crisis

- Access to talent and the best people

You must bear in mind that regardless of the results generated by the project, whether it goes well or poorly, it is not obvious that everyone in your organization knows about it.

Contrary to appearances, the management often forgets about activities that do not generate problems. Therefore, it may turn out that the board is well aware of the status of projects with frequent escalations and clashes with the clients but does not monitor projects that are conducted by the book. As a result, it may happen that the company's management has never met the project manager or the team that is succeeding and delivering excellent results. When such a project finally encounters problems, it turns out that getting anything done and receiving help is very difficult.

A conscious project manager should take care of relationships with key decision-makers within their own company.

A project manager must regularly talk to these people, convey key messages, share information about the team's successes, and sometimes even organize internal steering committees to present the deliverables and, more importantly, introduce individual project team members. This way, the project manager can effectively build support for the project and team, take care of their PR and visibility within the company, and prepare an appropriate foundation for emergency situations.

To sum up, from the very beginning of the project, you should work on building informal relationships and your influence for the future. You need to take care of that both on the client's side and within your own organization. It's your job to ensure that each member of the project team, each manager, director, or board member, has informal relationships with their counterparts on the client's side.

You must always remember that both the client and the vendor are organizations where individuals pursue their own agendas, and you do not run the project in a vacuum. It is your responsibility to navigate this situation effectively, move gracefully, and deliver the projects!

CHAPTER 12

Rule 5: Focus on Progress and Be Pragmatic

Be stubborn on the vision and flexible on the details.

—Jeff Bezos

Complicated, complex, or unrealistic projects cause stress and problems. They create situations and work conditions in which you need to make decisions based on facts and actual possibilities, and at the same time, remaining calm and objective is extremely hard. We tend to fall into the trap of tunnel thinking, taking into consideration only an available or convenient set of data. Most people don't function well under pressure and feel overwhelmed by the client's or management's demands.

It's difficult to stay professional and make smart and well-balanced decisions in this kind of environment. That's why, in difficult projects, we often see a certain level of emotional and irrational behavior, both on the client's and vendor's side, at every level of the management structure.

© Marcin Dąbrowski 2025
M. Dąbrowski, *10 Rules for Impossible Projects*,
https://doi.org/10.1007/979-8-8688-1463-1_12

Effectively carrying out the project requires a great degree of self-restraint when making decisions—you need to focus on the progress and be pragmatic at all times. So, every action needs to be focused on making progress in the project. Each situation has to be looked at from the point of view of progress rather than emotions, convenience or lack thereof, or comfort and security.

Good decisions, discussions, and solutions push the project toward completion. Oftentimes, they don't make you feel comfortable, bring about annoyance, knock you off balance, seem to add more work for you and the team, or take you out of your comfort zone.

Most discussions or conversations about what needs to be done in a given situation follow a repetitive pattern. Both sides exchange information about what each is responsible for instead of working together on the best solution. There is a problem to solve, a strategic decision to make, and suddenly, it turns out that everyone has their own duties and tasks, but no one feels obliged to take responsibility for moving things forward! In this way, problems remain unsolved for a long time, and progress is halted.

It is obvious that most of these types of problems lie at the intersection of the responsibilities of different people! Very often, the required solutions mean that individuals have to go beyond their scope of responsibility and make an extra effort.

It cannot be that individual team members later feel wronged because they were "forced" to perform tasks outside their area. Similar dilemmas arise when interacting with the client. You attend a meeting where someone articulates a problem lying at the boundary of the responsibilities of both companies and suddenly, there is silence. No one wants to take on the task of solving it.

Often, the situation is even more difficult. Namely, both sides subjectively interpret their responsibilities. This approach only leads to a stalemate, entrenchment of positions, and obviously to completely unnecessary delays.

The key criterion for decision-making and acting, both in the client-vendor relationship and within our team and company, should be project progress!

Everyone should ask themselves: "Am I contributing to the project's successful realization by acting this way, or am I only delaying it?" When leading a project, you should implement a work culture from the start, where the primary focus is the pragmatic pursuit of project success. By setting an example for our team and the client, you can, in a finite time, create a work environment where pragmatism and a proactive approach play a dominant role, where people do not ponder whether they are offended, whether someone has added extra tasks of those "other" people or the client, but focus on finding pragmatic solutions that are objectively beneficial for the project.

In one of the projects in Asia, the client struggled with defining the requirements for the necessary integrations with external systems. These tasks were, of course, within the scope of the client's responsibilities. At the same time, the vendor was developing and configuring the system according to the contract terms. The problem was that, from the client's perspective, the system was not useful since, without integrations, it didn't retrieve data necessary for the users' daily work.

As one might predict, a deadlock soon occurred. Initially, the vendor argued that they were fulfilling their contractual obligations, but after some time, they realized that the client would not accept the system and, thus, would not pay. Therefore, the only sensible solution to unblock the project was to go beyond the contractual terms, beyond their own scope of responsibility, and help the client. This decision was made, and soon, the project got back on track. Had the vendor acted pragmatically and focused on progress from the start, the situation wouldn't have escalated. Instead, regardless of who was to blame, both parties wasted time on polite exchanges about who was theoretically responsible according to what was stated in the contract.

You should aim to be pragmatic at all times. Especially while making tough decisions, in particular, those directly affecting individual members of project teams. In a project for a large European client, a conflict arose between the leaders of one of the project's areas. A person on the client's side escalated the issue, stating that they couldn't communicate with their counterpart on the vendor's side. The matter reached a high managerial level, where the client categorically and firmly demanded the replacement of the leader on the vendor's side. The problem was that the person they wanted to replace was a longtime, experienced, and respected vendor employee. They had excellent technical competencies and project experience.

Unfortunately, in this situation, there was a lack of so-called chemistry between them and their counterpart on the client's side. Continuous conflicts and lack of understanding were blocking the work, which the client rightly escalated. This person took the client's request very personally, further worsening the situation.

Ultimately, a decision had to be made. On one side, there was a deserving employee, a respected team member who somewhat demanded that the company protect them. On the other side, the client was pressuring the leader to change the project, which was at a standstill. In such moments, one must try to gain distance and think pragmatically. In this situation, the goal was to deliver the project. It was the client who commissioned and paid for the work of the team. The client had the right to demand the replacement of a given person. Therefore, such a decision was made. Of course, everything was carried out with respect to the mentioned team member, who ultimately took on a different role in the project, accepted the new setup, and, in the end, was more satisfied.

In all this, let's note that pragmatic decisions, good for the project, are very often difficult, uncomfortable, and initially even meet with disapproval from your own team. People appreciate this only after some time when they have understood that it couldn't have been done differently and when the positive outcome is clearly visible.

Thus, you should remain pragmatic while dealing with problems and making important decisions related to the scope, schedule, or quality. The lack of this pragmatic approach may lead to unnecessary delays. For example, it can take an indefinite amount of time to deploy the product, either due to performing the data cleansing before and after migration or to some functional defects, which usually take months to completely eradicate. If you and the client approach this issue pragmatically, it will turn out that not all the bugs are critical. First, you should focus on the critical elements, start the system, and then gradually concentrate on the less pressing issues.

Similarly, this applies to decisions concerning high-level project delivery strategy, splitting into particular phases, and replacing old systems with new ones. A perfect example of pragmatism is moving from the Big Bang approach to a more rational, phased implementation of functional areas.

Clients often design a strategy on paper to switch the entire group of IT systems to a new platform at one moment (commonly called the Big Bang). Then it suddenly turns out that the project's scope is too large, it cannot be logistically executed, there aren't enough competent people, and it's impossible for everything to be migrated at once. Such an approach might be enthusiastic but unrealistic. Interestingly, the project team, on both the client's and vendor's sides, must perform a massive task to convince both companies' management that the pragmatic and more rational approach to the project would be to extend it, divide it into stages, and in each stage focus on a selected and well-defined business area.

On one hand, this is the only sensible approach, as both companies can organize people and prepare for integration, migration, and change management. On the other hand, neither the client's nor the vendor's management like this. After all, the project was supposed to be completed faster. The vendor planned to invoice faster. It was supposed to be a huge success right away. **As always, pragmatic decisions are inconvenient and do not have many supporters.**

However, the project moved forward thanks to them, and we delivered.

You should avoid ideological approaches to solving problems and making decisions at all costs. The fact that something is written in the contract does not matter! The theoretical responsibility of the client (or vendor) according to the agreement should not concern us either. After all, these provisions were made perhaps one or two years in advance, when neither party was aware of the environment in which the project would be implemented and the challenges it would face.

Any kind of orthodoxy is the enemy of project progress! It causes unnecessary friction, introduces empty discussions that are merely a waste of time, and ultimately leads to conflicts.

Here, too, you should abandon the notion of "who is right" and be guided by pragmatism. Our goal is project execution, so you need to seek solutions that generate progress and bring us closer to our goal in the shortest possible way. It doesn't matter who is right, wrong, made a mistake, is guilty, or acted correctly. You must focus on what can work here and now rather than on theoretical or academic considerations!

Attempts to prove who is right lead nowhere! Not only are they meaningless and delay the project, but they also worsen relationships with the people we work with every day. This applies to both cooperation with the client and within your own team. If you engage in pointless arguments, you always lose: if you lose, you lose, and if you win, you also lose because you breed a new enemy, a person whose pride you have hurt. This is especially true if the discussion was conducted publicly, particularly in front of management. Being right does not add value to the project or interpersonal relationships! You should focus on finding solutions to problems so that work progresses quickly. No one cares if you win the argument or show someone your superiority. Contrary to appearances, bystanders perceive this as pettiness and immaturity, including the client's managers and your own.

Continuous fights and arguments call into question your own ability to communicate and cooperate with the team and the client!

In a large transformational project in Europe, there were regular delays against the schedule. The causes of the problems objectively lay on both sides. At some point, the project managers and entire teams on both sides entered a mode of mutual accusations, pointing out mistakes, proving guilt, and negligence. Theoretically, each of the teams was subjectively right to some extent. Sobriety came from the boards of both companies, which behaved very pragmatically and maturely.

Both project managers were asked if they could still work together. This question quickly brought their thinking back on track. They understood that the goal was to solve problems and complete the project, that the boards of both companies were tired of their rhetorical skills and would simply remove them from managing the work in the next step! No one cared who was right or who was guilty. Both companies needed a pragmatic approach to work and delivering the project.

Often, we tend to think that everyone is waiting to point out our mistakes. In practice, no one pays attention to it. What matters is the project's progress and not who was right, who was guilty, or who made a mistake! Therefore, discussions about it are pointless.

We should also remain pragmatic in relation to ourselves, especially in situations of stress, conflicts, or heated discussions. Nothing should be taken personally, and you should not get offended. Although it seems obvious, it is not easy to keep calm when the client or team members communicate aggressively, point out what was done wrong or what was not delivered, what we are responsible for, and so forth.

Taking such comments and discussions personally obscures the real picture of the situation and leads to emotional decisions rather than those that are optimal for project completion.

You must remember that every company has its own interests (different from yours), every person has their own goals and motives (both professional and personal), and every person has flaws and personal problems that affect what they say at any given moment. Private or subjective judgments, in most cases, do not change the current state of affairs. They do not usually introduce anything constructive in terms of solving problems either.

What should matter to you is the project's progress and making pragmatic choices. Therefore, you need to focus on objectively assessing the situation and feasible actions. You must extract only objective data and facts from all the communication noise, from subjective and even aggressive or offensive remarks of individuals.

You should also communicate in a way that does not attack other team members or—even more importantly—the client. This is to avoid putting people in a defensive mode, where they try to save face at all costs. Instead, you should focus on an open discussion about potential solutions.

The simplest way to achieve this is to always treat problems impersonally. Therefore, talk about the substance of the situation and the data, consider what works and what doesn't, and what we can do together as a team. Avoid finding those at fault, reproaching, or scolding. Each problem should be presented separately from the people or parties who theoretically caused it. Only in this way can we build an open culture where people do not avoid difficult situations, do not delay, are not afraid to talk openly about problems, and proactively seek opportunities to act.

After all, we care about the project's progress, saving time and reaching the goal as quickly as possible. In a given situation, no one is interested in who is to blame but whether and how the problem can be solved in the shortest possible time. Of course, it's worth doing a retrospective later, analyzing the chain of events to prevent similar situations from happening again.

Even then, however, you should be pragmatic and focus on learning, so work on examples without referring to specific individuals. Everything can be explained based on facts, specific causes, and undertaken actions. You do not need any characters for this, especially specific team members, who already know what they did wrong and will surely appreciate respecting their dignity.

It is worth conducting a simple experiment that clearly shows the impact of treating problems impersonally. At the next steering committee meeting with the client or meeting with the client's management, when delays or issues arise in the project, take the initiative and refer to the whole situation without mentioning who is to blame. The positive effects will be immediate, especially when someone from the client's side is responsible for the problem or delay.

First, your counterparts from the client's side will likely appreciate it immediately and start defending you. Second, the client's management, usually aware of the whole situation, will immediately notice your proactive, pragmatic, and constructive approach. This way, not only do you focus the discussion at the meeting on objective facts, data, problems, and solutions, but you also gain the dedication and respect of the client's team and their management, who additionally feel reassured when they see that both sides are cooperating instead of wasting time on pointless scapegoating.

All discussions should be treated as a tool for getting things done! They should always be approached pragmatically, focusing on what has a chance to work!

During these discussions, you need to demonstrate that your primary concern is the realization of the project and generating progress. The client must feel that you will do everything to deliver the project. They should see that you act professionally, concentrate on proactive problem-solving, and get results.

Throughout this, you should avoid thinking in terms of "us and them"! You should not fall into the trap of "defending our people" or the company at the expense of the project—it doesn't make any sense and, unfortunately, is a common occurrence. You need to strive to be objective and work based on data and facts, avoiding decisions driven by emotions or subjective impressions, especially those caused by stress or fatigue. Ultimately, the client always notices this and highly values it!

Being pragmatic and focusing on progress also requires making decisions promptly when needed and relying on bold actions despite stress or discomfort!

The fear of making decisions always causes project delays. There are no exceptions to this. Unfortunately, the more hierarchical the organization, the less entrepreneurial spirit, the less people feel responsible, the slower decisions are made, and the more people avoid them. It must always be borne in mind that avoiding decisions gives nothing. Time flies, and the problems remain the same! The fear of making mistakes often paralyzes people, and that's why they prefer to delay the moment of confrontation with difficult situations, hoping that either someone else will make a move or, with time, they will gather more data, making the probability of error zero. However, usually, any decision is better than none!

In a Western European company, a very large project was carried out involving three parties, three companies. Each of them had to adapt their internal IT systems to the newly designed business processes, which defined the way of cooperation between the three mentioned organizations after the launch. One of the companies played for time throughout the project, as the new IT systems were to improve control and oversight of the business activities for which it was responsible. Understandably, they feared the potential loss of revenue, expecting inefficiencies to be detected and the client unwilling to pay for activities that did not add value. The other two companies suspected that something was wrong, but no one wanted to confront it.

And so, time passed. After two years, the decision-making moment for the production launch finally came. A week before the steering committee meeting, when this decision was to be made, the manager of one of the companies finally lost patience and directly called the client's board members, informing them of their suspicions. Within a few days, the situation polarized. It turned out that the company in question not only delayed the project but also falsified its reports and integration test results. It came to light that they had not been working on implementing changes or developing their IT systems and were completely unprepared for the launch!

As expected, the production launch did not happen! The client had to find a new partner and integrate with their IT systems. As a result, the project was delayed by more than a year! All because of the lack of courage from the managers on the vendor's side, the client, and the third company, which did not want to admit that they had no intention of participating in a project that might worsen their financial conditions. Such a confrontation could have been brought about much earlier, but each party feared its potential negative consequences.

Waiting and avoiding making decisions leads to even greater problems and delays, which only worsens the situation. If a problem exists, it needs to be faced here and now!

In summary, you must first focus on progress and be pragmatic. This should guide you throughout the entire project in every situation. You need to concentrate solely on actions that add value, accelerate work, and solve problems. Your interest lies in delivering the project as quickly as possible and ensuring that the client achieves their business goals. You should act so that both the client and your team see that you strive to make objective, substantive decisions based on data and facts.

Finally, you must build a culture of openness where people are not afraid to talk about problems or challenges. To achieve this, you should always separate issues from individuals, treat the problems impersonally, and discuss them in the same manner.

CHAPTER 13

Rule 6: Exert Pressure and Use Your Position

Embrace bad news to learn where you need the most improvement.

—Bill Gates

Situations where the client avoids making decisions that are crucial for the further implementation of the project are very common. As a result, part of the work is largely blocked. The vendor tries to continue the project, but the lack of decisions causes continuous delays, which in turn significantly increases costs. Worse still, this works to the detriment of the client! The expected work results are delivered considerably later.

Sometimes, decisions are delayed by the client's project team, which cannot get the attention of their own management. Other times, people make mistakes and then hide the truth for fear of their positions. Sometimes, the lack of decision-making is deliberate, a conscious strategy by the client to save costs, forcing the vendor to perform the work and solve additional problems outside the scope of the contract. It also happens that the client's management has various constraints, including budgetary, administrative, legal, or political, and for these reasons, does not want to take responsibility, consequently avoiding decision-making.

© Marcin Dąbrowski 2025
M. Dąbrowski, *10 Rules for Impossible Projects*,
https://doi.org/10.1007/979-8-8688-1463-1_13

An example that illustrates this situation well is a project for a large European company. Both parties signed a contract that very vaguely defined the scope of work. As is usually the case, the situation developed according to a well-known pattern. Both the client and the vendor interpreted the contract clauses to their advantage, leading to regular conflicts, particularly causing significant cost increases and financial losses for the vendor, who, to deliver the results, was forced to develop more features and maintain a correspondingly larger team. On the one hand, the vendor tried to deliver, while on the other hand, demanded additional project funding.

Continuous discussions and disputes about what was within the scope and what has not delayed the execution of the work and caused objective delays. The situation could have been improved if both sides had agreed on the financial terms of continuing the project. Unfortunately, the client consistently avoided making decisions on this matter. The problem was that the client's management had budget constraints and wanted to avoid taking responsibility for increasing the project's budget.

Additionally, no one wanted to be accused of wasting the company's money later. As a result, the client accepted that the project would be delivered later, that it would be executed under continuous escalation conditions, and that some features would not be received. The vendor, in turn, had to deal with delays and additional costs. This arrangement was not beneficial for either party.

When the client continuously avoids making decisions, you must consistently exert pressure and use your position—it's the only remedy!

As aggressive as it may sound, by doing so, you are proactively acting in the client's and the project's best interest. The lack of decision-making harms the project and the client. When you exert pressure, the situation usually polarizes very quickly. People or companies must react. They must do something. They cannot remain passive and avoid responsibility.

In a project by a large integrator in Asia, the integrator conducted acceptance tests of the system delivered by the vendor but delayed signing the acceptance protocol, thus simultaneously preventing the invoicing of completed work.

After an unsuccessful attempt to reach an amicable agreement, on the day of handing over the product to the end customer, the vendor informed the integrator that they would not launch the system in the production environment, as according to the contract (and also obvious principles of cooperation ethics), the integrator should first sign the acceptance protocol and only then has the right to use the work results. Consequently, the integrator signed the acceptance protocol within a few hours!

They couldn't afford to lose face in front of the client. The production launch was meticulously planned for that specific day, and the client wouldn't have understood why the integrator delayed the formal acceptance of the vendor's work results if their quality allowed for commercial use of the system! This behavior would have been considered unfair and inelegant—causing significant reputational losses. The vendor's action may seem brutal, but let's note that the integrator acted unethically and against the fair principles of cooperation. Sometimes, you are forced to firmly use your position! There is simply no other way.

Remember also that **exerting pressure does not involve creating an unhealthy work atmosphere, using fear, or emotional blackmail. It means focusing on progress and constantly pushing for the project's realization. If you encounter a problem, you must react immediately. You cannot wait. Exerting pressure then means focusing on finding solutions here and now.**

You do not allow people within your team or on the client's side to avoid responsibility. In conversations or meetings, you do not agree to letting things slide or allowing silence to fall. You actively ask, probe the topic, fight, and seek solutions. Moreover, if a person is responsible for a part of the scope or functional area where there is a deadlock situation, you somewhat force them to do something about it.

Building pressure thus means stimulating people to take action and make decisions.

Exerting pressure should be done gradually and gracefully. Initially, by default, you should always lead by example, focusing on progress and asking about results, specific numbers, and data. During a status meeting with the client or team, people often discuss what they have been doing, but there are no specifics about what they actually achieved!

Anyone can report at any time how hard they worked and how much they did. The key is what concrete results were generated, whether progress has been made compared to the last meeting, and whether the work results align with the plan and expectations! Only that matters, and you must verify it continuously. Each time during a meeting, very precise questions must be asked so that everyone, absolutely everyone, has to show exactly what they achieved since the last report, what did not work out, why it did not work out, what problems they encountered, how they can be helped, and what they plan to do in the upcoming period.

A good practice is also to prepare appropriate tools to support reporting. These tools should somehow force team members on both sides to provide specific information that you care about. You should, therefore, insist on showing progress or delays relative to the last reporting period. It's not about people writing a lot. What matters is that they provide precise information concisely. If you allow a free description of the work status, you will often receive long, flowery, but inconclusive descriptions. You are not interested in what someone was doing but in what they did or did not do!

Another thing is exerting pressure on the client (and your team) to conclude discussions with specific agreements in the shortest possible time. Here, too, you should set an example of how to conduct conversations. You cannot engage in personal attacks, prove who is right, or enter into unnecessary and lengthy academic discussions. You need to push for concrete agreements. Every statement should result in something.

whether everything was proceeding according to the steering committee's arrangements. This technique works in an incredibly simple way. If individual managers commit to something in front of the client, they will then personally fulfill their promises.

However, you need to be very careful. This is a double-edged sword. If you organize a meeting with the participation of, for example, the CEOs of both the client and the vendor, and during it, it turns out that it was not necessary, that you were not prepared, that the issues could have been resolved without involving the top management, it can end very badly for individual members of the project team on both sides, including you. You can be perceived as pragmatic, effective, competent, and courageous, someone who does not fear conflict with people very high in the organizational hierarchy of both companies and someone who will risk everything to deliver the project. But, you can also quickly be labeled as incompetent, unprepared, and ignorant of how to manage a project and communicate with the client. It may be very difficult to overturn the first impression from such a meeting later. It might even end your "career" at the company.

So, if you want to exert pressure on management, especially on the company's board members, you must thoroughly prepare. You cannot leave anything to chance. In particular, you have to remember that everything must be agreed upon with the client's project team. You could say that such a meeting should even be "scripted" by the project managers on both sides. Very often, even the top management on the client's side may be willing to participate in preparing such a meeting because they are the ones who, first and foremost, want the project manager on the vendor's side to receive the appropriate support within their own company!

If you want to efficiently exert pressure to execute the project, activate the client to make decisions and push them to fulfill their obligations, you must learn to skilfully use your position.

There will be moments when you are forced to act firmly, remind them who is responsible for what, who should deliver what by a given deadline, and what the consequences of inaction and lack of decision-making will be. Ultimately, you work based on a signed contract, which obliges both parties to perform specific tasks.

You should not be afraid to use strong arguments. You should also not be afraid of formal communication such as official emails or legal letters. By behaving this way, the situation usually polarizes, and matters objectively move forward. Indeed, this involves a lot of stress and conflicts, but ultimately, both parties reach some agreement, and issues are escalated to decision-makers.

Throughout this process, you must maintain balance and ensure that you do not destroy the relationship with the client or with individual people. Always keep communication channels open, especially informal ones, with counterparts on the client's side, particularly with the management. The worst thing that can happen is to switch to written communication and stop informal conversations. There is a significant risk that the situation will get out of hand and the project will be halted!

This type of communication should be an exception, a departure from the norm, something you rarely use, a last-resort lifesaver.

You must not get used to this mode of operation. This cannot be your dominant style. Escalations, even if necessary, come at a cost. Used too often, they distort relationships, undermine trust, and irritate people, especially the client's management, who are forced to take action. No one wants to be cornered and pressured into making decisions, especially the client. Even if it objectively makes sense, even if there is no other choice, even if it is in the project's best interest, the client and their team will be irritated, and the escalations will leave a mark. **Thus, it's an art to manage in such a way that these escalations occur as rarely as possible!**

During the project, you should also ensure respect for yourself and your company! No one else will do this on your behalf.

If you let the client "push you around," it will only get worse! You must not agree to an unjustified increase in the scope of work without the consent of both parties. You cannot accept unrealistic expectations regarding the project schedule. Often, clients do not meet the deadlines for their tasks, yet they still expect the vendor to deliver. This must not be passively accepted. One thing is a proactive and customer-centric attitude, but both sides should maintain a certain level of business integrity and respect.

Clients can sometimes behave inappropriately and inelegantly during meetings, shout and complain, destroy any attempts at reaching an agreement, or make any arrangements. Clients can delay payments for months and not sign off on protocols for correctly delivered, accepted, and sometimes production-launched system components. You need to exert pressure and firmly use your position. Unfortunately, such situations will occur. Some clients or managers start showing respect only when they are treated firmly.

For example, one of the clients from Asia had been overdue for a long time with payments for correctly received project phases. Moreover, they were pushing for additional features outside the scope. They promised that if the vendor developed these additional features, the client would transfer the money for the phases already delivered and formally accepted! This was in a system already deployed on production and based on protocols and invoices that the client did not want to pay! Polite requests for payment of overdue invoices did not help. Calls, emails, and conversations also did not yield any tangible results. Finally, the client was informed that the vendor withdrew from the project and suspended the system maintenance service until payments were received for the correctly delivered and production-deployed system. As a result, the client paid the overdue invoices within a week!

What's more, such behavior never reoccurred. This example is not intended to encourage similar actions. They are neither client-friendly nor elegant—they cannot be the standard. However, sometimes there is no other way. There are certain fundamental principles of business integrity, and you must act in accordance with them. Unfortunately, there will be times when, to maintain respect for your own company, team, or yourself, you must act firmly, decisively, and boldly.

Some clients tend to commission work in an unofficial manner. At the same time, they do not want to send formal orders and demand that additional expectations be met for free. They can even resort to blackmail, such as blocking acceptances, avoiding formal approval of works, delaying payments, threatening penalties, or even taking you to court!

In one of the projects, the client had been pressing for additional work from the beginning. The problem was that the functionalities they expected were not within the scope of the contract. The vendor meticulously recorded all change requests, the cost of which at some point was estimated at several thousand man-days. It turned out that the client had poorly planned the project and wanted to cleverly adjust the scope without additional payments.

At the same time, the project was significantly delayed, which was an obvious and natural consequence of the client adding extra features. At some point, the client began to blackmail the vendor with penalties and court proceedings! Ultimately, when the vendor started demanding funding for out-of-scope work, it turned out that the client did not have the appropriate budget, so the project was terminated. The obvious mistake was delaying and postponing discussions about funding additional work. The project lasted several years, and both the client and the vendor lost time and money. In particular, the vendor should have set a clear boundary at the very beginning of the project, firmly communicating that they did not agree to implement additional features for free!

Avoiding such decisions never brings anything good. The problem not only remains unresolved but also grows over time.

Your primary goal is to execute the project, generate progress, and deliver results. Any delays caused by fear, avoiding responsibility, complex processes, bureaucracy, decision-making paralysis, lack of communication, and the like are harmful. They work against both the client and the vendor.

On the one hand, the client achieves the planned business benefits with delays and continues to bear the costs of inefficient business processes and old IT systems they planned to shut down. On the other hand, the vendor is exposed to delayed invoicing, unplanned financial losses, or prolonged engagement of key personnel who cannot be freed up for other equally important initiatives.

For this reason, sometimes taking a firm stand and polarizing actions is necessary. You must then exert pressure and use your position. You do this in the interest of the project, the client, and your own.

CHAPTER 14

Rule 7: Consciously Manage Information Flow

When you find yourself in a hole, the first thing to do is stop digging.

—Warren Buffet

In difficult, unrealistic projects, you struggle with a multitude of problems from the start. You have a hyper-ambitious schedule to meet, which is simply impossible to do. The client, however, has been assured that everything is under control. You likely have to create a large part of the product from scratch. The client thinks that the product is complete and just needs to be properly configured and deployed to production. Someone promised that your company is a specialist in the field, yet you have no one familiar with the topic. Your management team expects the company to make a fortune, but the project is making losses, so no one wants to provide you with the right people, and there is no approval to hire new ones.

© Marcin Dąbrowski 2025
M. Dąbrowski, *10 Rules for Impossible Projects*,
https://doi.org/10.1007/979-8-8688-1463-1_14

The fate of such projects hangs by a thread from the start. The client largely assesses the situation and the project's progress based on the information you provide. What would happen if you told the client directly what you think about how someone sold the project, made promises, and where you really are? The answer to this question is straightforward. The project would be stopped in a short time, and the contract would be terminated, likely with your fault.

From the beginning, you must remember that conscious and deliberate management of the flow of information is crucial for the project's success! You must always have a deeply thought-out and meticulously planned strategy for what, when, and on what topic you speak, write, or present!

It might seem counterintuitive, but in fact, this also works in the client's interest! After all, you are doing everything to ensure the project is delivered!

So, what is the most important thing in communicating the project's progress from the client's perspective? First and foremost, it is a sense of security. The client wants to be assured that the vendor is in control of the situation, knows what they are doing, and that even if problems arise, they have solved similar issues in the past and will do so again this time, so there is no need to worry. If the company has completed similar projects, it must have faced various crisis situations that likely repeat themselves. Why should this time be any different?

Second, the client expects a certain level of transparency in reporting progress, successes, delays, risks, and problems. They want to be aware that they have complete information so that they can react quickly and make decisions if needed. This sense of security and awareness of transparency is the foundation of trust between the parties.

From the vendor's perspective, there are two parallel and independent reporting planes: internal reporting and external reporting. The first focuses on the vendor's internal work progress, including all, even the smallest, issues and risks that may block the work. If the project manager does not know something, if someone has missed an important detail, or if a problem is not being resolved on an ongoing basis, the project is delayed, which cannot be allowed.

Moreover, the amount of information needed to manage the project internally within the vendor's organization is overwhelmingly greater than what the client would like to know. After all, you have many departments with which to collaborate. You have analytical work and various modules to produce, which are assigned to different teams, departments, or sectors in your company. You may also be hiring third-party companies. To coordinate all this, you need a very good internal communication plan, reports, and meetings with various teams.

External reporting is just a subset. The client is not interested in the status of things from the "behind the scenes" perspective. They do not want to know all the unnecessary information from their point of view. They are only interested in whether the project is going according to plan, what might put it at risk, what has been completed, and if and where both parties encounter problems. The client also understands that the vendor is dealing with a lot of issues on their side. However, this knowledge is usually not needed for anything and may even be harmful. The client wants to be informed about significant difficulties in project implementation, especially those requiring a specific reaction from them.

You should skillfully choose which piece of information and when to present it to the client. Selective information sharing is in the client's interest, especially in the case of very difficult projects or those on the brink of disaster.

You must continuously assure the client that you have control over the project and that they receive key decision-making data. Each redundant and unnecessary piece of information, even if provided in good faith, can only worsen the situation and undermine trust in your company. You must always be very careful about what and when you say or write.

Providing all internal information to the client is not only unnecessary but also dangerous! It is disadvantageous for both you and the client! It is simply unwise and reckless.

For example, if you have just started a project, you usually have a lot of problems forming a team. Some people are acquired faster. Others must be found within the company, and their availability must be negotiated with the managers of various departments. Still, other roles won't be found within the company at all; they must be sourced from the market. You receive the first workload estimates for individual system elements from business units that will produce those elements.

It will probably turn out that they are significantly higher than those assumed by the sales team at the contract-signing stage. In other words, the internal project status will be quite chaotic—resource shortages, potentially underestimated projects, and currently estimated delays. And all this at the beginning of the project!

If, at the beginning of the project, you pass this status to the client, they will likely conclude that you cannot manage, the vendor is unstable, disorganized, does not control the situation, and cannot be trusted, and then, in a short time, will stop the project and terminate the contract, probably even with your fault.

You should convey important information to the client at the given stage of the project!

All vendors face similar issues at every stage of the project. Following the previous example, all vendors have identical problems when starting the work and forming the team. Moreover, clients are also aware of this. They fully understand the vendor's situation because they also carry out internal projects that start in the same way.

Clients do not want to be stressed by a lot of internal information. They expect information that is thought-through and valuable!

Your role as a vendor is to solve internal problems, overcome all obstacles, and deliver the project on time! It is obvious to the client that at every stage of the project, you have a lot of internal problems. They chose you precisely to solve them. Otherwise, the client would produce the necessary IT systems themselves. They pay you to do the work for them.

So, you should convey information wisely and selectively, informing the client about what is important from their point of view at a given moment!

Status information is needed to make decisions that move the project forward. Informing about what may potentially happen in a year, two, or three, especially if at the given moment neither the client nor the vendor can do anything about it, is asking for trouble and each time adds another brick to the deteriorating image of the vendor who does not control the course of events.

If you keep talking about how the next phases of the project are difficult, that the client did not give you enough data and requirements to estimate the work, that there are no people on the client's side to work on the next stages, that their expectations are greater so the system will cost more and the work will take longer, at some point the client will stop the project!

The client wants the project to be completed. Therefore, you should inform them about how the current stage is going, what progress you are making, and what problems you have, and show them what you are doing to deliver this stage and how much you care. In most cases, this is sufficient information.

In conscious and deliberate management of the information flow, timing is crucial! You have to wisely choose the precise moment when you intend to give important and especially negative news.

Remember that we are constantly dealing with "unrealistic" projects, which are exceptionally difficult, have an overly ambitious schedule, are poorly sold, and are unprofitable. Their success is questionable from the start, with the client constantly irritated. What would happen to such a project if, from the beginning, during the sales process, you reported all possible risks and problems? Then, even the vendor wouldn't sign the contract!

If both sides had been aware of all the challenges awaiting them from the start, they would probably have had to halt the work right after starting! Interestingly, if you analyze the history of successful projects, you usually see that both sides focus on the current work, the current stage, and pragmatic delivery. These projects were also delayed, but they still ended successfully from the client's perspective.

The conclusion here is very simple. You need to focus on delivering, progress, and the here and now. Regardless of whether your project is ultimately more or less delayed, the more you deliver now, the more secure your position as a vendor is. You should focus your information policy on current work, challenges, problems, and risks. The client should see that you are doing everything to deliver.

For this reason, you need to carefully plan what, when, and how you communicate. The client's perception of the project largely depends on the information you provide.

Therefore, if the current situation is difficult, and you are struggling with problems, delays, and risks, why add fuel to the fire by informing them that this is nothing compared to what might await in the next stages in two to three years? This almost invites the client to stop the project before those problematic stages even begin. Besides, you are probably not even sure whether those risks and negative scenarios will materialize. Moreover, it's not only the client who might react nervously in such a situation. The vendor might do so as well!

In one of the projects, even before signing the contract, an initial analysis phase, known as the blueprint, was carried out with the client to accurately estimate the scope of work, possible schedule, and potential risks. The project manager on the vendor's side was supposed to prepare a summary of this information for the management. Since this person was still inexperienced, they wrote a very elaborate summary of all possible risks and potential problems. Reading this report, one might get the impression that the project could not possibly succeed! The vendor almost withdrew from the tender process. Ultimately, the contract was signed, and the project turned out to be one of the company's greatest commercial successes!

This perfectly illustrates that you should carefully consider what information you give to the client and your own management team. The more experienced the project manager and team are, the better they understand which risks might materialize, which problems will be resolved, and which will be difficult to handle, and thus, they convey information to the client and their own managers more consciously.

The ability to skillfully convey information is crucial, in particular for unrealistic, difficult projects! For example, in one project, both sides struggled with delays in the first stage. On the client's side, the pressure from the business was enormous. The client's IT department, responsible for the execution of the work, began to openly threaten to terminate the contract. The fate of the project hung by a thread. If, at that moment, nothing had been delivered, the vendor informed us that, apart from the delay in the first phase of the project, the following stages would also be delayed.

To an even greater extent, the contract would have been terminated immediately. Both sides focused on preparing a recovery plan for the current phase, which was eventually delivered. Interestingly, the scope of the system delivered in the first phase of the project was so valuable to the client that despite the subsequent stages never being realized, the contract was not terminated, and both sides continued to work together for years.

Remember that the risk of project termination decreases with each delivery. The more elements of a working system you deliver, the more you go live in production, the more stages you complete, the greater value the client will see, and the less inclined they will be to consider stopping the work and terminating the contract.

Keeping this in mind, you should adequately adjust your information-sharing strategy. Initially, focus on current tasks, deliver at all costs, and avoid unnecessary stress for the client by deliberating about what might happen in two years. Later, when you have delivered a large part of the system, when you have validated yourself in the client's eyes, when they see the value and are not inclined to terminate the contract, only then can you afford to be more open about future problems and risks.

In the case of complex and strategic IT projects, both the client and the vendor often deliberately add intermediate phases, so-called quick wins, even at the cost of extending the overall project schedule. This measure aims to generate quick successes that demonstrate to the client's organization that continuing the project makes sense and brings benefits. If the delivery intervals of individual elements of the system or platform are a year or two apart, regardless of whether such a work schedule is in accordance with the contract, the client's management and business users may lose patience and stop the project.

At that point, no one is interested in whether it aligns with the contract. The reasoning is as follows: you have been paying for a project for a year (or two), and no value has been generated. Nothing has been delivered. How do you even know the vendor is working on something? Therefore, a good practice is to add the said intermediate phases, the so-called quick wins, which address a specific problem on the client's side. Even if these are not complete elements of the target system, even if it is a very narrow subset of the functional scope, the positive impact on the client's perception of the project is immense.

The preceding strategy was effectively implemented in a very large and complex project for a European company. The initial project schedule was planned for three years. The scope of work turned out to be very complex. It included, among other things, the replacement of over twenty IT systems, which were to be replaced by a new platform. As a result, it was apparent after just one year of work that the project would take two more years, even under favorable conditions.

Furthermore, the initially planned phased deliveries would not have worked. Their scope was too large and required the synchronization of many work streams. Therefore, both sides agreed to introduce several intermediate phases. Specifically, the first tangible milestone was to integrate key data sources in the company and provide the ability to read them in the new platform. The client thus received potentially useless functionality to browse information in one place but still had to work with the old systems. The key point, however, was that both the client and the vendor could announce success by delivering a tangible part of the project scope.

Both sides then introduced many additional intermediate phases, and ultimately, the project was completed successfully. Although the project was delayed by over two years, meaning it took twice as long as initially planned, it objectively could not have been completed any faster. There were also no products of similar caliber from other vendors, nor would any of them have been tailored to the needs of this particular client.

Throughout this time, both sides suspected that each of the subsequent stages would be more costly and time-consuming than outlined in the contract, but they consistently focused on completing the current phase, on the here and now. In this particular case, the vendor and the client were so motivated to complete the project that they also adhered to the rule of deliberately managing the flow of information.

The project manager and the business owner on the client's side carefully planned what should be communicated, to whom, and when. They also regularly organized information campaigns and meetings with future users, during which they explained how the changes would proceed, when to expect which functionalities, why the project schedule was changing, what benefits the new platform would bring, and finally, why it was worth waiting longer. With such a conscious client and skillful communication management, practically any project can be completed, no matter how difficult and potentially hopeless the initial situation may be.

Managing the flow of information consciously and deliberately is a very important and incredibly pragmatic principle. You have often encountered criticism of such behavior, even indignation, in your work.

In one project, the management team almost led to a disaster and contract termination by trying to carelessly relay all internal information to the client. Subsequently, all these people left the company, a new, more pragmatic project manager was appointed, who began to consistently apply the preceding principle, and the project was delivered.

In another project, the situation was similar. Its manager was constantly in conflict with the vendor's management because, in his opinion, the client should be informed of all internal problems. This was very risky because the project was already significantly delayed, and every additional signal of an even greater lack of control would have led to contract termination. One of the directors then said, "The line between honesty and stupidity is very thin." This project manager also resigned. As before, a new one was appointed who approached communication management more maturely, and, as before, the project was successfully delivered. The client was grateful for such a professional approach.

Finally, in the third example, the manager of a very complex project returned every few weeks with a new delivery schedule, each time emphasizing how the overall project completion date was being extended. Instead of focusing on delivering the current stage, he concentrated on the completion date of the entire project, particularly on the phases that were yet to begin. When pressured to focus on delivering tangible results for the client here and now, this person also resigned. True to the pattern, a new project manager approached management pragmatically, particularly using a thoughtful approach to managing the flow of information, and ultimately, the project proved to be a great success for both the client and the vendor.

When managing difficult and complex projects, or even unrealistic ones, the main focus should be delivery! Moreover, the client also wants the vendor to be effective, to control the situation, and to deliver.

One could say that selective information sharing is controversial. Maybe so, but it brings results. Clients are paying for results, not lectures on principles and moralizing. As described, individuals who focus on theorizing about "how things should be" often burn out and resign.

Therefore, practical techniques should be applied, those that are "battle-tested," ones that may not be intuitive but are pragmatic, lead to project success, and serve the client's interests!

Deliberate information management is one of these principles.

CHAPTER 15

Rule 8: Take Care of the Project's Financial Condition

He who works all day, has no time to make money.

—John D. Rockefeller

Financial losses on a project can lead to its destruction, deterioration, or failure regardless of the chosen project management approach. If it consistently generates negative results, it ultimately leads to the drainage of talent or competent people, shifting them to other profitable projects, and eventually to delays, escalations, or even complete paralysis of the work. For a project to succeed, the vendor must have ensured revenues to cover the work costs.

Projects without adequate funding are seldom successful!

As an example, a company acquired a potentially lucrative contract with a prestigious client. The project was supposed to be big, innovative, complex, and interesting. It seemed like a long-term partnership. In fact, it looked really promising. The first two years were like a continuing success

© Marcin Dąbrowski 2025
M. Dąbrowski, *10 Rules for Impossible Projects*,
https://doi.org/10.1007/979-8-8688-1463-1_15

story. The client was satisfied with the outcomes. The vendor delivered and made a profit. Everything was going well until the client's budget was cut.

Over a period of several months, it turned out that the vendor could not afford to keep financing the work. The best people were moved to other projects (the profitable ones). Development departments also shuffled their priorities. As a result, it led to delays and conflicts with the client on the top management level. In the end, the project, which looked promising and could have been very beneficial for both the client and the vendor, was stopped for financial reasons.

The purpose of every company is to generate profits. Therefore, financial assumptions are cascaded down from managers on the boards through all levels of the organization. Every manager of any unit is nearly always assigned some annual performance goals. It is treated seriously. People take it personally. After all, their annual evaluation, especially whether they receive a performance bonus, depends on it. Thus, it is hardly surprising that in their actions, they strive to make optimal decisions regarding the annual profits of their department and, consequently, the entire company. Regardless of everything, from the vendor's point of view, the project's priority directly corresponds to the profits it generates.

Problems with revenues consequently lead to resource shortages, subpar staff, unfilled roles, prolonged analysis, delayed deliveries, and ultimately, low-level SLAs and a lack of willingness by the vendor to develop the system further.

Lack of financing or insufficient financing of the project nearly always leads to a significant deterioration of the project's situation, escalations, delays, and often to the end of cooperation. It works to the detriment of both the vendor and the client. Therefore, we must ensure the financial condition of the project at all costs!

For this reason, you should not feel embarrassed about openly discussing that a set of functionalities, in your opinion, is out of scope.

Under no circumstances should you avoid the conversation that the client should pay extra for it.

After all, these are additional costs that you must incur. Often, people fear such discussions. Business analysts or consultants, in particular, want to deliver the best system to the client that meets all their expectations, especially those they forgot to mention during the contract signing phase! But this is exactly how you estimated the project, offered a specific price, and signed an agreement. If the client asks for an additional feature, of course, they need it; it is valuable to them, and they cannot use the new system without it.

The problem is not that you don't want to deliver the feature to them. Of course, you do, but not for free! After all, if both parties forgot something or omitted certain objectives and requirements during the negotiation stage, it cannot be that now one side can recall this without consequences, but the other must dutifully deliver it, and for free!

Very often, discussions of this sort are embarrassing and leave a bad taste for both parties. Before the contract is signed, certain things are not yet obvious, but after a few months, these initial uncertainties become clear. It is difficult to explain to the client that the feature they are asking for is out of scope. After all, you know it is indispensable, and users cannot work efficiently with the system without it.

The core of the issue is not whether you think the feature is needed or whether the client is right. In most cases, the feature is needed, and the client rightly demands it. The question is whether the feature was part of the work estimate before the contract was signed or not!

If it wasn't, and if you didn't include it in the contract's scope of work, you must firmly insist that the client pays for additional work! From your perspective, it is an objective cost that was not planned or covered by the current project revenues. Unfortunately, you must proceed firmly—even if it is uncomfortable or mentally exhausting. You have two options. Either consistently maintain the project's financial health or choose the easier route and agree to the client's demands for free.

The first option involves a certain level of stress, temporary conflicts with the client, and discussions about what is in scope and what is not, but ultimately ensures funding that allows you to keep your company actively engaged in the project. This way, you still have the necessary team, financial means, and appropriate priority and respect in difficult situations.

The second option seems simpler and more comfortable, especially from the short-sighted perspective of the team working directly with the client. They don't have to fight with them. They give them everything they want. The client is satisfied, respects them, and treats them as friends. However, the problems accumulate because—day after day—additional features creep into the scope of work for which no one pays. As a result, the project's profitability begins to decline over time. Sometimes, the project even ceases to be profitable. Such situations end very badly for both the client and the vendor.

The wiser and more pragmatic approach is to regularly face a controlled level of stress and frequently open discussions about ongoing additional work and the corresponding necessary funding. If you avoid this, you are begging for disaster.

This is perfectly illustrated by an example of a European project, where many details and assumptions regarding the purchased IT platform were omitted at the sales stage. Nobody was to blame here. On the one hand, the client assumed that the offered product was complete, and thus, they did not specify their expectations. On the other hand, the vendor estimated the project based on the data provided by the client. After the work began, the client started noticing functional gaps and naturally pressed for the production of missing features.

From the vendor's perspective, these were additional tasks that had not been estimated. During the project, there were numerous reflections on how to proceed, whether to discuss this matter with the client or accept higher project costs. From the analysts' perspective, the client was right.

They expected the features that the implemented system should have. From the vendor's managerial perspective, the project's profitability was declining.

Ultimately, it turned out that the cost of the work was almost twice as high, causing several months of delays in each phase. As a result, after two years of the project's duration, the vendor's management found themselves in a critical situation. The client escalated significant work delays and continued to demand free implementation of their out-of-contract requirements under the threat of penalties.

At a certain point, when the vendor's management decided to confront the issue and summarize the additional cost of scope changes that the client should finance, the client halted the project and terminated the contract.

This is a perfect example showing that avoiding regular, controlled, but still stressful or uncomfortable discussions about financing change requests can lead to disaster for both the client and the vendor!

It is best to take care of the project's financial condition by actively engaging in the sales process. This is the stage where you can transparently discuss the scope, cost estimation of delivering the required features, delivery timeline, and the related payment schedule with the client. The more you clarify and agree with the client at this stage, the less stress your project will generate in the future. This way, you avoid potential disputes about what is in scope, what should be charged additionally, and any internal issues arising from insufficient project revenues.

What to do if the company consistently incurs losses on the project? In that case, you must push for renegotiation of the financial terms.

After all, if the project's results are negative month after month, quarter after quarter, or year after year, your company is effectively financing the client! In other words, the vendor is essentially paying for the client to gain business benefits from the results of their work. Of course, you can rightly discuss what led to this situation. Perhaps the vendor misquoted the project. Perhaps they deliberately underbid to win.

However, it is also possible that the client did not precisely specify the scope of work. Maybe their current expectations exceed the sales phase assumptions, resulting in the vendor having to incur additional, unplanned costs. There can be multiple reasons. This is described in my previous book, *Managing IT Projects.*

Without going into detail about how your project generates financial losses, the important thing is that you are running an unprofitable project and objectively need to think about how you can improve the financial conditions. Dwelling on history or finding the guilty party does not help. Even if you know that the project was misquoted or mis-sold, management will still rightly pressure for its execution, including making it profitable. Therefore, the only pragmatic solution is to renegotiate the financial terms! As previously described, if the vendor incurs losses on the project, it most often negatively affects the client.

Moreover, at the root of the problem is that you have more work to do, which increases the costs! Regardless of what both parties agreed upon during negotiations and contract signing, an arrangement where one party incurs financial losses due to the contract execution is unfair from a business perspective.

How can you start renegotiating financial terms? First, you should present the problem to the client objectively and explain why continuing work with the vendor incurring losses is detrimental to the project and the client.

You should explain how this will lead to constant conflicts, escalations, and delays, ultimately causing the client to incur losses, sometimes exceeding those on the vendor's side. You need to clearly outline the alternative scenarios for the situation, demonstrating that the suggested financial improvements can bring tangible business benefits to the client. This means the project will be executed with higher priority, better personnel, on time, and with the expected quality. This allows the client to deploy the system faster and shut down the old systems they continue to pay for. However, you ought to clearly show the risks of rejecting the vendor's requests to align revenues with the objectively higher costs of the work.

If the client's attitude is constructive, they act professionally and strive to be fair from a business point of view, the financing issue can be discussed, and a constructive agreement can be reached. For example, one of the projects carried out for a European company was generating losses. From the client's perspective, it seemed the vendor did not want to continue developing the system, which had just been launched commercially!

At the root of the problem were too low revenues, which meant that the vendor, having a limited team, constantly shifted people to more lucrative projects. They could not behave otherwise, as the goal of every company is to optimally manage resources to maximize profits. The client tried to threaten with penalties, but the vendor openly demonstrated that even if that happened, from an economic point of view, they could not act otherwise. So, the system's development on the client's side was effectively blocked.

Fortunately, the client's management was open to listening to the vendor's problems, understood the nature of the issues, and approached the matter in a very partnership-oriented manner. As a result of discussions and negotiations, the client agreed to increase the project funding. Consequently, the project manager on the vendor's side had the proper arguments to secure a team for further work.

Unfortunately, it may turn out that the client is not constructive, trying to gain as much as possible at all costs. If their strategy revolves around minimizing expenses and maximizing the vendor's use, then the matter becomes more complicated. In such cases, building pressure and quickly resorting to formal communication is necessary.

The most important thing is to make the client clearly understand what might happen and the alternative scenarios—showing what is objectively better for them and what risks ignoring the vendor's financial problem might entail.

Ultimately, the vendor may be forced to limit losses and halt the project (temporarily or permanently) or even withdraw from further contract execution. Then, the matter will most likely end up in court, or both parties will reach some form of agreement and establish terms for an amicable separation. In both scenarios, the biggest loser is the client. If the vendor is so desperate as to stop the project, it is natural that they have thoroughly considered their decision and find this course of action optimal from their perspective.

On the other hand, this is often the worst possible scenario for the client. First, they lose the time spent selecting the vendor and then implementing the project up to the present day. Second, they have incurred work costs, and during this time, they have been paying to maintain the old systems that were to be replaced. Third, they must choose a new vendor, which will most likely pay them much more than the additional payment requested by the previous vendor!

Therefore, if you are managing a project that is generating significant financial losses for the company, and if the client refuses to take a constructive approach to the problem if they are deaf to your requests, you must first make them understand what such behavior can lead to and what the consequences will be.

Of course, such a strategy only works if the client, at least to some extent, makes decisions based on facts and business logic. Unfortunately, this is not always the case. For example, the vendor attempted to renegotiate the financial terms during the implementation of a long-term project that generated losses year after year. After several rounds of meetings and discussions, there was no prospect of a positive resolution. Therefore, the vendor informed the client that they would not extend the annual contract for further development and maintenance of the implemented IT platform due to the losses incurred.

Only then did the client realize what this meant: they would have to spend years searching for and implementing a new product, pay several times more, and still not have any guarantee that the new system would be as good as the current one. Ultimately, the vendor accepted the proposed financial terms. It should be emphasized that the client primarily followed business logic. They analyzed what was more profitable from a business standpoint. Individual managers had the proper authority and decision-making capabilities.

Unfortunately, this is not always the case. In another example, the situation was very similar—a long project regularly generating losses on the vendor's side, who desperately asked for a change in financial terms. In this case, however, the client's organization was more rigid and highly procedural, and individual managers mainly focused on avoiding mistakes and keeping their jobs. They also could not make decisions based on business logic. Procedures and processes were more important than the financial data. Consequently, both parties quickly reached the stage of discussing the termination of cooperation.

You must remember that it is not always possible to improve the financial condition of a project. There are contracts signed in such a way that you have no room for maneuver. Some clients are deaf to substantive arguments. There are some people with whom you cannot reach an agreement. Sometimes, you have to let go. If the client does not want to understand that the vendor cannot continue to incur financial losses and finance the work if they do not want to listen, they will be the biggest loser in the event of a split. This is likely what will happen. There is nothing you can do about it. Unfortunately, sometimes processes, procedures, or internal politics overshadow business logic and common sense.

Regardless of whether the projects are interesting, innovative, or even revolutionary, and regardless of the added value they bring from the client's perspective, they can still fail due to financial reasons on the vendor's side.

No company can indefinitely finance work. A project that generates losses must always have a lower priority within the organization, leading to resource shortages, delays, escalations, conflicts, and sometimes premature project termination and the parting of ways. Therefore, if you want your project to be successful, if you want to run it under the right conditions, and if you want it to have the right status within the company, you must ensure its financial health from the very beginning!

CHAPTER 16

Rule 9: Create and Document Your Own Project History

All you have in life is your reputation.

—Richard Branson

Each time you start a new project, you think that success is guaranteed if you stick to the contract to the dot. Besides, we're taught that what matters most is the scope, time, and quality. Students are told that during their IT studies. And then this message is reinforced by all sorts of training courses. It is also said in many coursebooks, including those that help prepare for the certification examinations in project management. So, if you deliver the scope within the agreed timeframe and with the required quality, you're bound to be successful. Unfortunately, this approach is very childish and naive.

It turns out that any project can be stopped by the client at any time, no matter how diligent you are or how good your intentions are, regardless of whether the project is conducted according to the contract.

© Marcin Dąbrowski 2025
M. Dąbrowski, *10 Rules for Impossible Projects*,
https://doi.org/10.1007/979-8-8688-1463-1_16

So, let's have a closer look at the following three examples.

One multiyear and correctly managed project was halted due to organizational changes on the client's side. There was a change in the key personnel within the company. This, in turn, led to the emergence of new managers responsible for the project. As often happens, the managers in question wanted to separate themselves from the decisions and choices of their predecessors. They halted the project and brought in new vendors and top-tier products. They applied a common but conservative strategy in line with the well-known saying, "Nobody got fired for buying IBM."

In other words, they signed a new contract to implement products from such well-known vendors that, even if the project ultimately failed, no one could blame them. After all, if such companies couldn't deliver the project, no one else could. The problem was that this reasoning had nothing to do with the original vendor's performance. The vendor had virtually no means of defense. The project was simply phased out within a few months.

Another time, a project was halted right after the formal acceptance of the first stage, which had been worked on for almost two years. The client had neither formal reasons nor legal possibilities to terminate the contract. Up to that point, no critical remarks had been raised either. There were no conflicts or escalations. This decision came as a huge surprise to the project teams on both sides, especially on the client's side! As it turned out, the company was about to be acquired, and to increase its value, the financial director was halting all investment activities that could potentially be cut, thereby reducing the company's operational costs. It is obvious that if the newly implemented platform had not fully replaced the old IT systems, the project could be stopped without major consequences for the ongoing business. Time and money invested so far are lost. However, in this situation, it did not matter. As before, the client's decision was unrelated to the vendor's deliverables. No matter how well the project was managed, it would have been stopped for the reason described.

In the third example, the vendor successfully implemented a large part of the system in production. It was also a great success for the client! The key business objectives of the project were met. From the vendor's point of view, a lucrative period of maintenance and further development of the newly launched system began. Unfortunately, within a year, another company took over the client, which had a completely different strategy for IT tools development. New vendors and systems were then introduced. This happened even though the vendor was fulfilling the contract, and the client was satisfied!

The preceding examples were meant to show that any project can be stopped at any time. This can happen regardless of the outcomes of your work, even if the tasks are performed by the book and in accordance with the contract terms, even if you are delivering the expected and tangible results.

Unfortunately, the mere fact of stopping the project is not the end. In the next step, clients most often try to blame the vendor for the project's failures and negotiate the best possible financial terms for themselves.

They try to impose penalties, withhold payments for correctly issued invoices, or take the matter to court to demand even greater compensation for the alleged losses. Let's look at the following examples, which illustrate this pattern of action.

Let's start with the mildest of them. In this case, the client abruptly halted the work after successfully completing the acceptance tests. Then, they stopped communicating and responding to contact attempts and consistently rejected invoices for the correctly delivered project stage. When the vendor began formally demanding their rights and threatened to take the matter to court, the client proposed a settlement to amicably conclude the project and part ways. The entire situation was caused by the client's financial problems. Unfortunately, they needed to reallocate the budget to other, more critical projects and thus were unable to pay the vendor for their work. As a result of the settlement, the client paid only a small portion of the due invoices. They could not, however, accuse the vendor and seek compensation in court because there was solid evidence that the project was being carried out according to plan, especially since the acceptance tests had been successfully completed.

The second example looks at the project described at the beginning of the chapter, in which the client's financial director halted all initiatives that he considered unnecessary expenses and reduced the company's potential value before the planned acquisition. Following the pattern, the client first quietly stopped the work, ceased communication, and consistently avoided payments for the correctly issued invoices. However, he did not officially terminate the contract because the project history documentation did not allow him to do so. Documents, presentations, emails, and protocols showed that the project was carried out according to the contract. As before, the case ended with a settlement in which the client again paid only a portion of the due invoices.

Finally, the last example shows the worst possible scenario. In this case, the client underestimated the project costs and, when they realized this, officially terminated the contract and then took the matter to court, seeking reimbursement of costs. They accused the vendor of delays, imposed maximum penalties, and made additional financial claims. The court appointed an expert who thoroughly investigated what led to this situation in the project. After several years, it turned out that the client could not prove any fault on the vendor's part, so the accusations were withdrawn, and the parties signed a settlement. The vendor defended themselves mainly because they consistently documented all significant facts during the project, and the gathered documentation was so reliable that the court expert rejected the client's charges and arguments.

The client's intentions are as follows: after terminating the contract, they usually try to shift the blame to the vendor and negotiate the best possible exit terms. This strategy only works if the vendor does not have an appropriate means of defense. That is why, from the very beginning, you should prepare for the possibility that the client may terminate the contract and try to hold you responsible for reasons beyond your control.

You must consistently build facts documenting your subjective version of the project's course. You need to create your own "project history." Then, you must repeatedly communicate it and reach every person on the client's side. Specifically, you need to communicate it to the client's management and the board. At the same time, you must document everything continuously to have materials for defense in case of the worst-case scenario, such as termination, court proceedings, or negotiations of separation terms.

From the beginning of the project, you ought to create and document your own project history.

By doing so, you can do the following.

- Consistently defend yourself against the politics played by hostile individuals on the client's side or the competition.

- Build defensive arguments in case the client wants to threaten you with penalties.

- Build arguments and favorable facts if the client wants to force you to perform additional work for free.

- Gather arguments and facts in case the client wants to terminate the contract.

- Prepare arguments and facts for the fight during the negotiation of financial terms after the client terminates the contract.

- Ultimately, build reliable evidence to defend yourself in court.

First and foremost, you should realize that the client largely evaluates the vendor and the project's outcomes based on the information you provide and opinions overheard during informal backstage conversations.

Therefore, from the outset, you should consciously create and maintain the PR and image of your company and project. Contrary to appearances, this is not difficult at all. You just need to slightly embellish the narrative at the right moments, positively and subjectively describing the progress of the work. You should highlight and emphasize all, even the smallest, project successes while omitting failures.

As bad as it may sound, you should also, as much as possible, attribute successes to your company and blur the responsibility for problems, particularly documenting all the mishaps of third parties and the client. Remember, your intention is not to act to the client's detriment. This way, you are prepared if the client behaves unfairly toward you, suspends the project, terminates the contract, and takes your company to court despite you delivering the work according to the contract! Unfortunately, there is no other way.

Later negotiations of separation terms show that often both parties heavily embellish. To defend against this, you must document your subjective version of the project history in advance, presenting the delivery in a positive light. Let's go back, however, to the period when you are executing the project.

First and foremost, you must build and disseminate a positive image of the project according to the preceding advice. You should do this in project meetings, steering committees, informal conversations, during coffees, lunches, or joint integration outings with the client. Remember, if there are any hostile individuals in the client's organization, they will take every opportunity to complain, malign, distort facts, spread pessimism, and show how wonderful it was with the old system and how the new one won't meet expectations.

Similarly, third parties, especially competitors, act in the same way. Sellers and consultants from other companies do not waste time and do not have mercy. They are constantly trying to sell competing services and products. They do not hesitate to make negative remarks about you, bring up your failures from this or other projects, and paint a great vision of the project with their own companies. If, at the same time, you do not counteract this, if you do not actively take care of the positive PR and image of your project and company, it gradually deteriorates.

In one of the projects I personally participated in, the CTO and board member on the client's side said to our team: "Other vendors spend 20% of their time working and 80% on marketing. Conversely, you spend 80% of your time working and only 20% on marketing. As a result, few people in our company realize how hard you work and how much you have already delivered. Do something about it!".

Of course, this is not about taking this statement literally and focusing on building an image at the expense of substantive work. However, it should strongly make you realize that creating your own subjective project history and then communicating it to everyone, especially decision-makers, is very important!

Moreover, most project managers have probably experienced a meeting where the client's management came to the meeting hostile and reprimanded the vendor, even though they were not to blame. Why did this happen? Someone talked to these managers earlier. Someone told them their version of events. Someone prepared them for this meeting. A few such meetings and the client may conclude that the vendor is not performing as expected! Therefore, continuous work on the image of your project and your company is necessary.

At the same time, you must document your subjective project history!

Whatever happens in the project, good or bad, it does not exist from the perspective of future court proceedings or negotiations if it has not been "put on paper."

Your biggest successes or failures will have no significance in the future if they are not documented. For example, in one project, the head of procurement on the client's side boasted that he had never lost a case against any vendor and, for months, tried to blackmail the vendor to deliver extra features for free. The vendor, on their part, meticulously documented all additional work and registered the work hours of all team members with precision. When the client indeed took the matter to court, it turned out that the vendor presented very strong documentation of additional work and detailed costs of each team member's effort day by day. The client, however, submitted their claims and costs on just two pages.

Consequently, their charges were ultimately dismissed. The lesson is very simple and clear. If you systematically document your version of the project's history, you can feel relatively safe when the client terminates the contract, makes baseless claims, and takes the matter to court.

Therefore, you should document all the project's significant facts or events, especially those that validate your subjective version of the project's history.

These can be small or big successes, like completing analytical work, solving a key problem, finishing tests, and moments when the client praises you for something or thanks you. Above all, you must highlight all additional actions you have taken to help the client.

Conversely, do not forget to document all mishaps by the client or third parties. If the client ever accuses you of causing delays in the project, you must be able to show that it was not your fault or at least that the client contributed to them. If you do not document the delays, problems, or shortcomings on the client's side, the expert or judge will never know about them. During a court trial, no one will benevolently admit to their negligence. That's why you must document them regularly.

It's also important to point out that documenting is not the same as secret journaling for its own sake. Your job is to "generate facts," which later become history. Each record in the documentation is only valid legally when you can prove that the client knew about it. The most valuable materials are documents, presentations, meeting minutes, or emails the client confirmed, approved, or cooperated with you. As a bare minimum, you need to be able to prove that the client was made aware of the particular piece of information and did not reject or oppose it. Sometimes, an email is enough, even if the client just received it without responding.

You need to remember that documenting facts is not that simple. For obvious reasons, clients or third parties take good care of appearing blameless in the future. That's why you may often encounter a problem where individuals on the client's side deny that a negative incident occurred, particularly that they were to blame. It may seem ridiculous at first, but then you often end up in a situation where you want the project manager on the client's side to confirm the meeting minutes in which it is stated who caused the delay or a standstill in a given area. They reject the notes and cross out the unfavorable part even though it is true. That's why the facts should be documented in a deliberate, clever, and impartial manner.

People dread personal responsibility and desperately avoid records pointing to "the guilty party." They, however, agree to a dry, matter-of-fact way of documenting facts or events.

So, instead of writing that a particular individual failed to deliver on time, it's enough to state that a particular element of the scope will be delivered at a later date. You have no interest in blaming a specific person. It's important that it is possible to determine in the future who was responsible for delays in a given area, whether it was the client or the vendor. Thus, if you have a contract that clearly defines the accountability of each party and impartial records documenting the project events, you can easily determine whether a particular delay was caused by the client or by a third party. And no records refer to particular members of the project team.

Creating, continuously telling, and documenting your own subjective project history is essential.

First, it allows you to carry out work, guide conversations in meetings, and build a positive image of the project and the company in the eyes of the decision-makers. At the same time, it protects you from the hostile actions of some individuals or companies that try to undermine your efforts and distort reality to bring the project to a halt. Also, meticulous documentation of all key facts and events happening from the time of signing the contract is your only line of defense if the client terminates the contract and makes claims for damages either in court or in negotiations.

That's why you need to create and document your own project history.

Even though this work is tedious, it seems a waste of time, and people avoid it. This habit may be invaluable for the company, the project, and you.

CHAPTER 17

Rule 10: Focus on the Long-Term Relationship with the Client

It's all about the long term.

—Jeff Bezos

The project that you're currently running is just a stage in your relationship with the client. We tend to forget that. There are challenges and risks that we need to face every day. There are tens of meetings every week or even every day. You need to coordinate the efforts of multiple teams, including those on the client's side. A lot of tasks are delayed. There are open discussions with the client. And in all that havoc, both the management of your own company and the client expect that that work will be delivered on time. It's difficult to stay cool-headed and think strategically in an environment or climate like that. The timeframe you're focused on is often the deployment of the current project stage.

© Marcin Dąbrowski 2025
M. Dąbrowski, *10 Rules for Impossible Projects*,
https://doi.org/10.1007/979-8-8688-1463-1_17

If you care about the relationship with the client, the cooperation may last several years or even longer. You can keep selling your products to them, even those that don't exist yet; there may be a lot of projects to come!

That's why you should focus on building a long-term relationship with the client from the very beginning and adjust your actions accordingly when making decisions.

By looking at the relationship with the client from this perspective, you can clearly see that your understanding of the project, priorities, and the things that really matter to the client and to you has changed dramatically. You stop dwelling on minor issues. All of a sudden, any fights and struggles, proving the other party wrong, ensuring that you are in the right in every meeting, and trying to win at all costs are pointless.

If you treat the relationship with the client strategically and you want to maintain the relationship for years, you start asking yourself what attitude you should be displaying. What makes you and your company so special that the client will want to continue working with you? Effectiveness and delivering outcomes are important.

What truly matters, however, is your attitude, how you treat the client, whether you are proactive and helpful, whether you try to solve problems, whether the client feels safe with you, whether they trust you, like you, and want to cooperate with you.

There are plenty of examples of situations when the client returns to the vendor to extend the implemented solution, commission a new product, or carry out another project to solve some other problems. It is all based on the interpersonal relations and the company image created during the previous cooperation. Someone remembers you, the fact that you did your best, were helpful, professional, and worked in a way that added value. The people you work with are often promoted or move to other companies, but they still remember you!

Interestingly, in retrospect, it does not matter to them if the previous projects were delayed, hard, or caused problems. People mostly remember your attitude and the way they were treated. So, even if the project was delivered "by the book," but you as an individual or as a company acted in a selfish, arrogant manner and blamed the people on the client's side, then despite the timely completion of the project, you should not count on any recommendations in the future.

If, on the other hand, there were plenty of problems in the project, it was very delayed, the meetings with the top executives or even the board were necessary, you worked under a lot of pressure but managed to behave respectfully while interacting with the client's representatives, you were determined to help and defend those people and in general, worked as one team these people will remember you forever!

You could say that the closest relationships with the client and certain individuals are built in the most difficult projects, but only if you treat those people with respect and act proactively and in a pro-client manner.

Your attitude matters not only for the individuals that you work with but also for the client's management team. In every organization, managers, regardless of the level of hierarchy, pursue order and stability. They care about selecting vendors that their team will like and want to work with. So, if they know that the members of their team respect the vendor, that they find them trustworthy, that they feel comfortable, and that they will be able to deliver results without any major conflicts, escalations, or havoc, the manager in question will be open to work in the same setup again. It will just make them feel comfortable and safe. That's exactly why you often lose contracts in sales processes in favor of the "preferred" vendors whose products might be worse and whose competencies are lower, but the client knows them, trusts them, and wants to work with them.

While conducting projects, you should, therefore, aim to nurture the relationships with the client so that they last long, and the current project is just the first or next stage in a longer-term venture with the client.

That said, it's often either forgotten altogether or a sad reality that pushes people to act in ways that are strategically suboptimal. If the project generates losses, the management tends to forget about the prospects of future cooperation with the client and long-term plans. What counts is the financial results here and now. Thus, the organization can risk its relationship with the client to improve the project's annual revenues. Similarly, individual managers may try to optimize work in a way that allows them to get the best financial results possible at the cost of deteriorating some particular, often promising, projects that are not generating satisfactory profits. When acquiring a new contract, vendors may also neglect current clients. That way, you risk losing a promising business with valuable clients due to some short-sighted activity.

Toward the end of a project for a European company lasting several years, the client decided that the system that had already been implemented would be replaced with a new one. As they decided to buy a product from someone else, the current vendor decided not to do business with this client anymore. Assuming that there was nothing to lose, they raised their service rates as high as possible to make a profit while the project still lasted. As you can imagine, it was the last project ever for this particular client.

In another example from the same region, a promising relationship with the client was built. A complicated program was being run. The cooperation was smooth until the time came to deploy the systems that had been developed as individual projects. The client needed extra support, performing extra tasks for which they didn't have the budget at that time. The vendor had two options. One of them was to lose money in the current year and get the benefits from developing the existing systems and then make profits resulting from developing the implemented systems or to negotiate the extra pay here and now, exert pressure on the client, and give them no choice but to pay extra. The latter option was chosen. As a result, before the program finally finished, the relationship between the management team and some individuals on the client's side was effectively destroyed. Within several months, the cooperation between the two businesses was irrevocably harmed.

There are also some positive examples in which the team's and the entire organization's right attitude resulted in long-term cooperation with the client. For example, one project was supposed to last two years and finished after eight years. A system was being implemented that was supposed to be a complete product, but in reality, it had to be developed from scratch. The project team didn't manage to prevent escalations. There were some heated debates and stress for individuals both on the vendor and client side. There were some financial struggles, of course. There were delays, penalty threats, negotiations, and so forth. In all this, the client was always treated respectfully. During conflicts and tough situations, the project teams always acted in a professional and proactive manner. Nobody was offended. Nobody was blamed. Eventually, the system was deployed to production but was delayed for several years. The project was completed. During the project, some people made friends and built close relationships that have made it to this day.

Another much bigger project conducted abroad was run in a similar way. Instead of one and a half years, it lasted five years. A product was sold, but it didn't yet exist. A contract that specified the scope of work was signed. After some years, the system that was delivered was much different from the one that had been initially commissioned. Stress, escalations, working for 12 hours a day, or even at the weekends were common occurrences. The project was severely delayed but was deemed a great success after all.

Like in the previous example, despite the hard conditions, the client was treated with respect, the work and conversations were conducted in a professional manner, both teams focused on facts, and a proactive approach was displayed. And the outcome? Individuals on the client's side still reminisce about that period with a sentiment. Most team members built long-lasting friendships with their counterparts on the client's side. Moreover, some of them later went on to work for other companies, but they kept recommending the vendor as a trustworthy partner and invited them to participate in bids.

That's why you can't look at a project as a venture that ends with the acceptance protocol. You should work and make decisions in such a way that the project is the first or next step in the relationship with the client, the step that precedes the following chapters about the cooperation between both businesses.

So, how do you act so that it becomes real? There are two basic elements that you should pay attention to.

- The attitude you present throughout the project

- The way key decisions are made on the team and company level

So, let's start with attitude. Once again, we come back to the fact that you should be proactive and pro-client, try to get out in front, and solve as many problems as possible, especially on the client side, even those outside the scope of the contract. We need to be professional, work with facts, avoid personalizing our frustrations, avoid blaming individual people, try to work as one team on the client and supplier side, defend the client against their own management, offer solutions, push forward, attack problems transparently and head-on and finally show that we are trying to deliver at all costs what the client cares about. All this seems obvious, even elementary, even simple and easy.

The difficulty, however, is to behave in this way at all times, that is, even when the customer resents you, even when the customer stigmatizes you, accuses you, blames you, makes personal comments, makes it difficult to meet, undermines agreements, avoids making decisions, when your management resents and accuses you, when either the customer or your managers intimidate or threaten you with the consequences of delays, when you have to work at weekends or nights when particular tasks or people annoy you, and so on. It is easy to read or write about it, but it is much more difficult to keep a cool head and an iron will when we are in the "heat of battle."

Still another issue is decision-making. This subject is much more difficult because it usually involves your entire company, including the board of directors. All decisions within the project, or decisions about the project, should, therefore, be analyzed from the point of view of strategic, long-term cooperation with the client. You should avoid making decisions dictated by emotions, under the influence of momentary difficulties, or in terms of annual company results or perhaps the bonuses that individual managers would like to receive here and now.

In theory, the issue seems obvious, but is it really? The problem is not with straightforward decisions but with beneficial ones in the short and long term. Difficulties and dilemmas will arise when a company has to accept a financial loss on a project in a given year to make money in the following years or when it has to sacrifice profits in other profitable projects to keep a team on the project, which is currently not profitable. It will also be a problem when the client demands more than what is written in the contract, when you have to choose between sticking firmly to the contract and making additional investments, incurring additional costs to keep the client happy and wanting to work with you in the future.

It also happens that the client takes away some part of the project scope and gives it away to third-party companies. You can act emotionally and, in your resentment, block such actions (and you usually have the means to do so), or you can calmly accept the client's new strategy, show that you support them no matter what, and consequently work with them for several years longer.

Finally, when a client decides to switch off your system, instead of blocking this and trying to earn as much as possible "while we can," you should still behave professionally and look for new opportunities to work together. It is important to remember that the people we work with on the client side are not always responsible for the decisions that are difficult for you to accept. Sometimes, they make them against their will. Therefore, it is not worth venting your frustration on them, making their lives difficult and obstructing them. You gain nothing by doing so and can only lose more.

So, no matter how difficult the situation you find yourself in as a team or a company, you should analyze every decision from the perspective of the long-term relationship with the customer, from the horizon of the next few years (not months!).

You must act based on facts, data, and factual assessment of the situation and avoid being driven by emotions at all costs.

Running complicated, complex, unrealistic, or theoretically impossible projects involves constant stress, uncomfortable decisions, escalations, conflicts, heated debates, working after hours, and fatigue. In such an environment, keeping your distance and thinking ahead is difficult. So, let's remember the last rule of delivering impossible projects.

From the start of the project, focus on the long-term relationship with the client!

Consider how the client will remember you, how they will describe your cooperation years later, what they will say about you to other potential clients, whether they will recommend you, and so on. Finally, think about what is important to you. Do you want the current project to be the last one you complete for this client? Or do you want it to be the beginning of a long-term, fruitful cooperation in many areas?

CHAPTER 18

Conclusion

It's kind of fun to do the impossible.

—Walt Disney

To conclude, I would like to go back to the beginning—to the purpose or point of writing this book. Well, it is very easy to run projects that are simple, well-defined, perfectly sized, reliably estimated, sold at a fair price, and with a client who is understanding, patient, well-meaning, and perfectly organized. Under such conditions, everything we have learned in our studies or training, all the project management theory, and the knowledge we have gained during the certification process is completely sufficient and works well.

It is completely different when you run difficult, complex projects, or projects that have been delayed from day one, projects that have been inappropriately sold and do not have sufficient financing, projects where we lack competence, people, where clients build up pressure, are disappointed, threaten to impose penalties or terminate the contract.

In short, projects that, for the purposes of this book, I have defined as unrealistic or impossible are projects that, in all probability, have no chance of success. In such projects, even your own company seems to work against you! In situations like this, project management theory is rarely effective. For example, no matter how long you keep lecturing the managers of the various departments that you have a specific contract

© Marcin Dąbrowski 2025
M. Dąbrowski, *10 Rules for Impossible Projects*,
https://doi.org/10.1007/979-8-8688-1463-1_18

and schedule and need to deliver on time, they remain completely deaf to your preaching. Your project is making a loss, and they won't involve more people.

You can also try to explain to the client that the scope of work they expect cannot objectively be delivered on the expected date. But the client may reply that they signed a contract that says that the project has to be delivered earlier. So, even though you want to act according to the highest project management standards, the client and your own managers do not listen to your reasoning.

In an environment like this, you can't rely solely on theory and known methodologies. It's just not enough. Projects like this are possible to complete, but only if you consistently apply the practical knowledge that I put in the following 10 rules.

---

10 Rules for Delivering Impossible Projects

Rule 1: Get involved in the contract negotiation.

Rule 2: Define what it means to "deliver" the project.

Rule 3: Be helpful and show commitment.

Rule 4: Build relationships and the power of influence.

Rule 5: Focus on progress and be pragmatic.

Rule 6: Exert pressure and use your position.

Rule 7: Consciously manage information flow.

Rule 8: Take care of the project's financial condition.

Rule 9: Create and document your own project history.

Rule 10: Focus on the long-term relationship with the client.

If you apply these rules in practice, you greatly increase the likelihood of your projects succeeding. By the way, it's hardly surprising. These rules are a result of combining the knowledge from years of running difficult, unrealistic projects, which we mostly managed to complete despite their hopeless condition. You also need to remember that each project, each client, and each contract are different. That's why you should use these rules thoughtfully. The list is by no means a decalogue that you should blindly follow.

Some of these rules or some parts of particular chapters may seem counterintuitive and awkward. They may stand in opposition to what is taught in training courses or project management schools. For example, in regards to the second rule—define what it means to deliver a project, I once got a comment saying, "While the pragmatic approach seems understandable, it's difficult to accept that what was written in the contract is supposedly meaningless." It is, and it isn't at the same time.

You should avoid orthodoxy in anything you do, even when it comes to the rules presented in this book. It goes without saying that signed contracts have to be respected. It is also obvious that you need to strive to deliver what was agreed in the contract. But what if the contract was written inappropriately? What if the client didn't fully understand their needs when the requirements were defined? What sense does it make to follow the provisions of the contract, then? Where does it lead? Does the client want it in the first place?

The aim of the "Define what it means to deliver the project" rule is not to undermine contracts. Its aim is to inspire you to regularly inspect what is important to the client or even what is the most important thing if you have to choose. And yes, it often turns out that the client defines success differently than what was specified in the contract signed several years before when the client didn't have enough data to specify their expectations properly.

197

During a conversation with my friend, I heard that he had a problem with "rule 7 about consciously managing information flow." And I agree. It is not an intuitive rule. The most natural reaction for anyone is to talk openly. But if you think for a moment and become pragmatic, you will conclude that it's better to focus on the outcomes and the consequences of your actions for the client, the project, and your company.

The client wants the project to be completed. They want to believe that the vendor has the project under control. They want stability and a sense of security. Informing the client about all the problems that you are currently facing is just unreasonable. The project manager might think that they are the last man standing, but in fact, the client's and the vendor's management treat them like a person who is honest but naive and inexperienced.

I personally witnessed a situation when someone told the project manager that there was "a thin line between honesty and stupidity." And then, as you can imagine, the management demanded a replacement. And yes, the project manager was right in theory. But in practice, he was removed from the project and lost all control over it! It's not about avoiding conversations about problems altogether. Of course, you need to talk about them!

However, there's a difference between talking about pragmatic solutions to deliver the project's current phase and constant warnings that you have no clue whatsoever about what will happen in the upcoming phases, that the work is underestimated, and the project will surely be delayed. If you keep spreading negativity and sharing bad news with the client, the project will likely fail—mostly because the client will stop it!

Your goal is not to be right, act according to some theoretical principles or blindly follow the guidelines of any methodology just for the sake of it. Your goal is to complete the project for the client. That's why you should be pragmatic and follow rules that are effective and work in practice.

A great exercise in this area is to analyze challenging projects that were eventually successful. It's worth looking at them closely and talking to all the people involved. It is especially good to ask them about their most difficult challenges and how they were solved.

By doing this exercise, you will see that the rules described in this book were applied in projects like this, especially the extremely difficult ones. Surely, maybe just a subset of them, or they were used in some part, but they were still applied. Unfortunately, it mostly happened intuitively, based on the experience of some individuals. What if you don't have this experience? What if you're not lucky enough to have an experienced person on board? The project's success cannot be left to a lucky coincidence!

I think that practical knowledge should be available to everyone. Why struggle for years, learn from mistakes and failures, and risk your reputation and career if you can just spend a few hours reading this book? I hope the rules described in this book will help you deliver projects for your clients.

Good luck!

Index

A, B

Build relationships/power of
    influence, 117

C

Client's definition, 38–40
Contract negotiations
    acceptance criteria, 84
    approval process, 84
    business unit managers, 82
    change requests (CRs), 78
    critical error, 86
    delays and problems, 75
    demands/expectations, 87
    draconian contracts, 85
    financial loss, 89
    hostile environment, 90
    interdisciplinary team, 88
    key account manager, 80
    lucrative phase, 78
    payment schedule, 81, 82
    penalty charges, 83
    potential penalties, 83, 84
    preparation/negotiation stage,
        77, 78, 86, 88
    quotation and negotiation
        process, 79

D

Delivering project
    bidding and negotiation
        process, 101, 102
    Big Bang strategy, 97
    budget/timeframe, 96
    client's goals/
        expectations, 96
    conciliatory project, 94
    contract definition, 93, 94
    contract terms/project
        triangle, 105
    criteria and project
        delivery, 105
    data extraction, 95
    definition, 97
    friction/escalation, 100
    international constellation, 95

© Marcin Dąbrowski 2025
M. Dąbrowski, *10 Rules for Impossible Projects*,
https://doi.org/10.1007/979-8-8688-1463-1

M, N, O

P, Q, R, S

T, U

V, W, X, Y, Z

GPSR Compliance
The European Union's (EU) General Product Safety Regulation (GPSR) is a set
of rules that requires consumer products to be safe and our obligations to
ensure this.

If you have any concerns about our products, you can contact us on

ProductSafety@springernature.com

In case Publisher is established outside the EU, the EU authorized
representative is:

Springer Nature Customer Service Center GmbH
Europaplatz 3
69115 Heidelberg, Germany